MORE SPECIAL REQUESTS

100 FAVORITE RESTAURANT RECIPES FROM THE PAGES OF THE

ST. LOUIS POST-DISPATCH

D1376981

Editor
Judith Evans

Art Director
Tom Borgman

Photo Editor
Hillary Levin

Proofreader
Frank Reust

Sales and Marketing
Cory Parolin-Doehler
Angie Clark

Cover Photographer
John L. White

ST. LOUIS POST-DISPATCH STAFF PHOTOGRAPHERS

David Carson 69, 173, 177, 179
Robert Cohen 165
Stephanie Cordle 27, 169
Dan Eldridge. 9, 59, 95, 119
Karen Elshout. 29, 161, 185, 203
F. Brian Ferguson. . . . 49
J.B. Forbes 7, 151, 189
Jason Fritz 19, 113
Elie Gardner 13, 15, 57, 99
Max Gersh. 87
Christian Gooden 25, 47, 73, 125, 127, 129, 167, 191, 201, 205
Sam Leone 93, 103
Erik M. Lunsford. 121
Huy Mach 71, 109, 171, 175
Dawn Majors. 53, 77, 79, 85, 97, 101, 123
Odell Mitchell Jr.. . . . . 105, 115
Jerry Naunheim Jr.. . . . 55, 107, 197
Teresa Prince 159
Emily Rasinski 17, 37, 81
Laurie Skrivan 155
John L. White 35, 61, 63, 117, 139, 141, 143, 145
Brittanie Williams . . . 11, 147, 149, 181, 183, 195

FREELANCE PHOTOGRAPHERS

Don Adams Jr.. . . . 43
Katherine Bish . . . 89, 163, 199
Rod Boren. 39, 45
Sarah Conard 23, 33, 41, 51, 67, 193
Whitney Curtis . . . 21, 31, 75, 111, 133, 135
Kyle Ericson 187
Sid Hastings 91
Mike Kurlowski. . . 153
Tom McCarthy Jr. . 65
Becca Young 83, 131, 137, 157

ISBN 10: 0-9842084-3-7
ISBN 13: 978-0-9842084-3-2
Printed by Walsworth Publishing Co., Marceline, Mo.
To order additional copies, call 877-767-8785. Order online at: www.thepost-dispatchstore.com

INTRODUCTION

Welcome to a taste of St. Louis.

We've gathered a wide array of recipes, each shared by a generous chef, from restaurants of all descriptions. Whether you'd like to replicate something on the menu of a fine restaurant or try your hand at an ethnic specialty, you'll find a recipe here.

Chefs often cook in great quantities and by feel – a handful of this, a few pinches of that – rather than using measurements. Mary Billings, who writes the Special Request column that appears weekly in the Post-Dispatch, has tested each of these recipes and adapted them so they work in home kitchens.

Enjoy!

Judith Evans
Food Editor
St. Louis Post-Dispatch

SNACKS AND STARTERS

7.. Shrimp Scampi........................... Anthony's Bar
9.. New Orleans Style BBQ Shrimp............. Truffles
11.. Coquilles St. Jacques .... Chez Leon
13.. Cha-Cha Calamari........................ Sage
15.. Coconut-Steamed Mussels................ Boogaloo
17.. Queso Manchego en Adobo............... Modesto
19.. Goat Cheese Rarebit...................... Schlafly Tap Room
21.. Chicken Spring Rolls...................... Bugatti's Steak and Pasta (Ameristar)
23.. Chicken Liver Mousse..................... Revival
25.. Sweet Potato Salsa....................... Bleeding Deacon
27.. Bruschetta.............................. Harry's Restaurant and Bar

SALADS, SOUPS, SIDES AND SAUCES

29.. Pear Salad with Cherry Balsamic Vinaigrette.. Pestalozzi Place
31.. Grilled Green Bean and Smoked Tomato Salad. Square One Brewery
33.. Chopped Veggie Salad..................... Grafton's Landing
35.. Bambino's Salad.......................... Bambino's
37.. Broccoli Slaw .... Cardwell's at the Plaza
39.. Cream of Zucchini and Carrot Soup......... Gelato's Italian Ice Cream
41.. Carrot-Ginger Soup....................... Minions Café
43.. Chef Bob's Squash Soup................... Aggie's Closet and Tea Room
45.. Cream of Mushroom Soup................. The Mississippi Half Step
47.. Potato Soup .... Kenrick's Meat Market and Catering
49.. Old-Fashioned Navy Bean Soup............ Missouri Athletic Club
51.. Southwestern Chicken Soup .... JackSons'
53.. South Texas Tortilla Soup................. Canyon Café
55.. Lobster Bisque .... Brio Tuscan Grill
57.. Lobster Mac and Cheese .... Lucas Park Grille
59.. Corn Soufflé .... Highway 61 Roadhouse
61.. Crescent City Creamed Spinach............ Ruth's Chris
63.. Vanilla Sweet Potatoes.................... Sunset 44 Bistro
65.. Red Beans and Rice .... Blueberry Hill
67.. Tangy Pit Beans .... 17th Street Bar and Grill
69.. Brandy Peppercorn Sauce .... Citizen Kane's

MAIN DISHES

71.. Stir-Fried Spicy Eggplant .... P.F. Chang's
73.. Spinach and Gruyère Quiche ..... The London Tea Room
75.. Artichoke Quiche .... Magpie's
77.. Noodle-less Lasagna .... Sqwires
79.. Broccoli Lasagna .... Miss Aimee B's Tea Room
81.. Pasta With Broccoli............ Madison's Cafe
83.. Pasta Portobello a la Lilly .... Candicci's
85.. Pasta Primavera .... Tony's
87.. Rigatoni all'Amatriciana .... Roberto's Trattoria
89.. Bow-Tie Jack Pasta .... The Hawthorne Inn
91.. Shrimp Pasta With Vodka Sauce .. Mangia Italiano
93.. Alfredo Grill Pasta .... Alfredo Grill
95.. Chicken Pasta Fra Diavolo .... Brio Tuscan Grill
97.. Southwest Chicken Pasta........ Roxane
99.. Chicken Emil .... Rich and Charlie's
101.. Chicken Sorrentino............. Trattoria Branica
103.. Chicken Marsala .... Fratelli's Ristorante
105.. Chicken Amaretto.............. Marciano's
107.. Chicken Spiedini .... Rizzo's Pasta
109.. Enchiladas de Crèma .... Arcelia's
111.. Cayo Chicken................. Wapango
113.. White Chicken Chili........... Big Bear Grill
115.. Grilled Chicken and
      Mushroom Risotto .... Sofia Bistro
117.. Triple Mustard and
      Pecan Chicken Salad .... La Bonne Bouchée
119.. Chicken Salad .... Shrine Restaurant
                                    (Our Lady of the Snows)
121.. Curried Chicken Salad .... Tea Room in the Valley
123.. Chicken Salad Pie............. Miss Aimee B's Tea Room
125.. Pistachio-Crusted Ruby Trout .... Kitchen K
127.. Pan Bagnat (Tuna Sandwich)..... Franco
129.. Shrimp Pan Roast.............. Pearl's Oyster Bar (Ameristar)
131.. Bacalao a la Vizcaina .... Guido's Pizzeria and Tapas

MAIN DISHES CONTINUED

DESSERTS AND BAKED GOODS

SHRIMP SCAMPI

ANTHONY'S BAR > 10 South Broadway • St. Louis • 314-271-7007

YIELD: 4 APPETIZER SERVINGS

8 tablespoons (1 stick) butter, divided

3 to 4 tablespoons fresh bread crumbs

2 cloves garlic, pressed or minced

16 large (16- to 20-count) shrimp, peeled and deveined

1 tablespoon chopped fresh parsley

½ cup Chablis

¼ cup peeled, seeded, sliced tomatoes (see tester's note)

Salt

Ground black pepper

Crusty bread

Preheat the oven to 450 degrees. In a medium skillet, melt 1 tablespoon butter over medium heat; stir in bread crumbs. Toss until butter is absorbed and crumbs are slightly browned. Transfer crumbs to a plate.

Melt remaining 7 tablespoons butter in the skillet; add garlic. Add shrimp. Cook about 4 minutes, turning once or twice. Add parsley and wine; simmer 3 to 4 minutes. Add tomatoes; season with salt and pepper to taste.

Pour into an oven-safe serving dish. Sprinkle with bread crumbs. Bake 5 minutes or until bubbly. Serve with crusty bread.

Tester's note: Firm plum tomatoes (sliced or minced) work well in this recipe. For a slight variation, add 1 teaspoon drained capers with the tomatoes. The crumbs on top serve both to decorate the finished dish and to slightly thicken the sauce. For a main dish, serve the shrimp and sauce over pasta.

Per serving:
260 calories
23g fat
80% calories from fat
15g saturated fat
104mg cholesterol
5g protein
3g carbohydrate
0.5g sugar
no fiber
70mg sodium
26mg calcium
108mg potassium

NEW ORLEANS STYLE BBQ SHRIMP

TRUFFLES > 9202 Clayton Road • Ladue • 314-567-9100 • trufflesinladue.com

YIELD: 4 SERVINGS

1 tablespoon freshly
squeezed lemon juice

1½ teaspoons plus ¼ cup Lea
& Perrins Worcestershire
sauce, divided

1 tablespoon paprika

2 tablespoons minced parsley

1 pinch dried thyme

1½ teaspoons coarsely
ground black pepper

¾ teaspoon ground white
pepper

1 dash Tabasco sauce

1 dash ground red (cayenne)
pepper

1 cup (2 sticks) unsalted
butter, slightly softened

2 tablespoons vegetable or
peanut oil

15 to 20 large (10- to
12-count) shrimp, peeled
and deveined

1 to 2 tablespoons Creole
seasoning, to taste (see
note)

1 bunch green onions,
chopped fine

French bread, for serving

Combine lemon juice, 1½ teaspoons Worcestershire sauce, paprika, parsley, thyme, black pepper, white pepper, Tabasco and cayenne pepper in a food processor; process until well mixed. Transfer to the large bowl of an electric mixer; add butter, a small amount at a time, beating at low speed until well-mixed. Refrigerate until very cold.

Heat a large sauté pan over very high heat; add oil. While pan is heating, season shrimp liberally with the Creole seasoning. Add shrimp to hot pan; do not move shrimp for 30 to 40 seconds. Then stir shrimp constantly until almost cooked through, about 2 minutes. Add remaining ¼ cup Worcestershire and green onions, then remove from heat. Add seasoned butter to taste a little at a time, stirring quickly. Serve with hot French bread to soak up sauce.

Note: To make Creole seasoning, mix together 2 tablespoons kosher salt, 2 tablespoons ground black pepper, 1 tablespoon garlic powder, 1 tablespoon onion powder, 1 teaspoon dried thyme, ¼ cup Hungarian sweet paprika, ¼ teaspoon ground red (cayenne) pepper and 3 bay leaves, finely crushed with mortar and pestle. Store in a sealed container. YIELD: ABOUT ⅔ CUP.

Per serving:

318 calories

30g fat

85% calories from fat

16g saturated fat

101mg cholesterol

6g protein

6g carbohydrate

3g sugar

0.5g fiber

492mg sodium

46mg calcium

220mg potassium

SNACKS AND STARTERS

SALADS, SOUPS,
SIDES AND SAUCES

MAIN DISHES

DESSERTS AND
BAKED GOODS

COQUILLES ST. JACQUES AUX ÉCHALOTES

CHEZ LEON > 7927 Forsyth Boulevard • Clayton • 314-361-1589 • chezleon.com

YIELD: 2 APPETIZER SERVINGS OR 1 ENTREE SERVING

---

1 tablespoon olive oil

6 large sea scallops

Salt

Ground black pepper

2 tablespoons minced
    shallots

¼ cup white wine

2 tablespoons white vinegar

¼ cup heavy (40 percent)
    whipping cream

2 tablespoons unsalted
    butter

1½ teaspoons chopped
    parsley

Heat oil in a small sauté pan over medium-high heat. Season scallops with salt and pepper to taste and place in pan; cook on one side about 3 to 4 minutes or until golden.

Turn scallops; add shallots. Cook for about 45 seconds. Add wine and vinegar, scraping the bottom of the pan with a wooden spoon to release the browned bits. Continue cooking until liquid is reduced by half, about 4 minutes. Add cream; cook until reduced by half.

Remove scallops to serving dish; keep warm. Add butter and parsley to pan; whisk until butter is melted. Spoon sauce over scallops and serve.

Per appetizer serving:

348 calories

30g fat

78% calories from fat

15g saturated fat

103mg cholesterol

14.5g protein

5g carbohydrate

no sugar

no fiber

170mg sodium

48mg calcium

279mg potassium

CHA-CHA CALAMARI

SAGE URBAN AMERICAN GRILL > 1031 Lynch Street • St. Louis • 314-256-1203 • sageinsoulard.com

YIELD: 6 TO 8 SERVINGS

1 cup buttermilk

5 (3- to 5-ounce) calamari
  steaks, cut into ¼-inch
  strips (see note)

Salt

Ground black pepper

1 cup all-purpose flour

1 cup cornstarch

Vegetable oil, for deep-frying

About 1 cup Thai Chile Aioli
  (see note)

Pour buttermilk over calamari; season with salt and pepper to taste. Cover and refrigerate 1 hour.

In a shallow bowl, stir together flour and cornstarch. Drain calamari and add to flour mixture; toss in a colander to remove excess coating.

Preheat an oil-filled deep-fryer to 365 degrees. Fry calamari in small batches to prevent sticking; cook for 1 minute, 15 seconds. Do not overcook, or calamari will be unpleasantly chewy; it should have the same tender texture as cooked scallops or shrimp. Drain; season with salt and pepper to taste.

Quickly toss with just enough Thai Chile Aioli to coat the pieces lightly. Serve hot.

Note: Look for fresh calamari steaks at good seafood shops. They are sold frozen at some supermarkets.

To make Thai Chile Aioli: Whisk together 1 cup mayonnaise, 3 tablespoons Asian hot chile oil, 1 tablespoon minced green onion, 1 tablespoon minced fresh cilantro, 1 tablespoon minced fresh parsley, 1 tablespoon minced fresh basil, 1 teaspoon minced fresh mint, 1 teaspoon salt and ¼ cup Thai sweet chile sauce (sold in Asian markets). For better flavor, let stand at room temperature 30 minutes before using. If preparing ahead, refrigerate; return to room temperature (do not heat or microwave) before adding to hot calamari. Refrigerate leftovers.
YIELD: 1½ CUPS
Per tablespoon: 81 calories; 9g fat; 160mg sodium.

Per serving (based on 8 servings):

389 calories

29g fat

67% calories from fat

4g saturated fat

214mg cholesterol

15g protein

17g carbohydrate

1g sugar

0.5g fiber

376mg sodium

49mg calcium

254mg potassium

COCONUT-STEAMED MUSSELS

BOOGALOO > 7344 Manchester Road • Maplewood • 314-645-4803 • boogaloostl.com

YIELD: 4 TO 6 SERVINGS

1 tablespoon vegetable oil

½ cup diced red bell peppers
   (in ¼-inch pieces)

½ cup diced onion

½ cup diced celery

2 tablespoons minced garlic

4 pounds mussels, cleaned

Salt

Freshly ground black pepper

1 cup white Sangria, Riesling
   or other sweet white wine

1 (13-ounce) can coconut milk

¼ cup chopped cilantro

Crusty bread, for serving

Heat a very large pot over medium heat; add oil, peppers, onion, celery and garlic. Cook until soft, about 5 minutes. Add mussels and salt and pepper to taste; sauté 1 minute.

Increase heat to high. Add wine, coconut milk and cilantro; cover and cook until all the mussels open, about 5 minutes. Lift mussels from liquid and divide among serving bowls, discarding any mussels that do not open. Cook liquid a few minutes more to reduce it slightly. Ladle broth and vegetables over mussels. Serve with crusty bread.

Per serving (based on 6 servings):

276 calories

17.5g fat

57% calories from fat

12g saturated fat

26mg cholesterol

13g protein

10g carbohydrate

1g sugar

1g fiber

285mg sodium

48mg calcium

517mg potassium

MORNING GLORY QUICK BREAD

THE DAILY BREAD BAKERY AND CAFE > 11719 Manchester Road • Des Peres • 314-909-0010 • thedbcafe.com

YIELD: 2 LOAVES OR 11 MUFFINS

½ cup golden raisins

2 cups unbleached all-purpose flour

1 cup granulated sugar

2 teaspoons baking soda

½ teaspoon salt

2 teaspoons ground cinnamon

½ teaspoon ground ginger

2 cups shredded carrots

1 apple (such as Gala), peeled and coarsely chopped

½ cup sweetened flaked coconut

½ cup chopped walnuts

⅓ cup sunflower kernels

3 large eggs

⅔ cup canola oil

2 teaspoons vanilla

Coarse sugar, for optional garnish

Preheat the oven to 375 degrees for metal pans, 350 degrees for glass pans. Grease two 3½-by-6½-inch loaf pans (see note), or four 3-by-5-inch mini loaf pans or 11 muffin cups or insert paper liners.

Put raisins in a small bowl and cover them with hot water; allow to soak while preparing the rest of the recipe.

Sift together flour, sugar, baking soda, salt, cinnamon and ginger into a large bowl. Stir in carrots, apple, coconut, walnuts and sunflower kernels.

In another bowl, beat together eggs, oil and vanilla. Add to flour mixture and stir until evenly combined. (Mixture will seem dry; keep stirring to make a thick, chunky batter.) Drain raisins and stir into the batter.

Spoon batter into muffin cups or loaf pans; sprinkle with coarse sugar, if desired. Bake until center tests done (a thin knife or wooden pick inserted in the center comes out clean). Crust will be dark brown. Baking times are approximately as follows: 2¾-inch muffins, 20 minutes; 3-by-5-inch mini loaves, 30 minutes; 3½-by-6½-inch loaves, 40 minutes. Cool 5 minutes before removing from pans.

Note: If using the more commonly available 4-by-7-inch pans, reduce the oven temperature to 350 degrees after 25 minutes.

Per muffin:

417 calories

21.5g fat

46% calories from fat

3g saturated fat

58mg cholesterol

6g protein

50g carbohydrate

27.5g sugar

3g fiber

379mg sodium

36mg calcium

253mg potassium

TRADITIONAL ENGLISH SCONES

PORT ST. LOUIS was located in Frontenac.

YIELD: 6 SERVINGS (SEE NOTE)

2 cups all-purpose flour

4 teaspoons baking powder

¼ cup (½ stick) cold butter

2 tablespoons granulated
   sugar

1 teaspoon vanilla

⅔ cup milk or more as
   needed

Whipped cream, for serving

Jam, for serving

Preheat the oven to 400 degrees.

Sift flour and baking powder together into a medium bowl. Use a pastry blender to cut butter into flour mixture until very fine. Stir in sugar.

Stir vanilla into ⅔ cup milk, then pour slowly into center of flour mixture. Mix in gradually with a fork, adding milk as needed to get a moist dough. Do not overwork dough.

On a well-floured surface, knead dough lightly, 2 or 3 times. Press dough with fingers to a thickness of ¾ inch. Using a 1¼- to 2-inch biscuit cutter, cut out scones. (Do not reroll extra dough, or scones will be tough.) Arrange on a baking sheet. To ensure that the bottoms do not brown, place the baking sheet on a second sheet before baking.

Bake smaller scones about 8 minutes; bake larger scones about 10 minutes. Scones are done when tops appear dry; do not overbake.

Serve warm or cold with whipped cream and jam.

Note: This recipe, which yields 12 larger (2-inch) or 18 to 20 smaller (about 1¼-inch) scones, is easy to double or cut in half. Add an herb of your choice to make a savory version, or add raisins or chocolate chips for a sweet variation.

Per serving:

253 calories

9g fat

32% calories from fat

5g saturated fat

23mg cholesterol

5g protein

38g carbohydrate

5.5g sugar

1g fiber

338mg sodium

220mg calcium

88mg potassium

POPOVERS

TEA ROOM IN THE VALLEY > 505 Meramec Station Road • Valley Park • 636-225-4832 • tearoominthevalley.com

YIELD: 24 MINIATURE POPOVERS

3 cups all-purpose flour

1 teaspoon salt

6 eggs

3 cups milk

3 tablespoons melted butter

Preheat the oven to 400 degrees. Spray mini popover pans (see note) heavily with nonstick cooking spray; set aside.

Using a whisk, stir together flour and salt. In a separate bowl, beat eggs until well mixed; stir in milk, then melted butter. Add egg mixture to dry ingredients. (Batter will be like thick cream.)

Fill pans ⅔ full. Bake 30 minutes or until golden brown. Popovers may be frozen after they have cooled.

Note: Mini popover pans are shaped like truncated cones. They can be found at kitchen specialty stores.

These are easily removed from well-sprayed nonstick bakeware. Avoid using lightweight, shiny aluminum tins.

Per popover:

104 calories

4g fat

35% calories from fat

2g saturated fat

60mg cholesterol

4g protein

13g carbohydrate

1.5g sugar

0.5g fiber

127mg sodium

44mg calcium

78mg potassium

DESSERTS AND BAKED GOODS

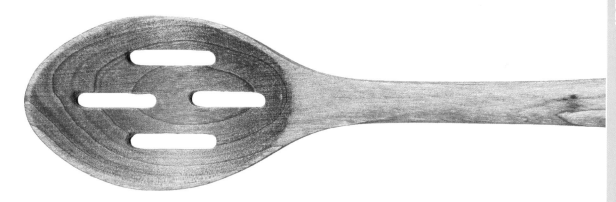

QUESO MANCHEGO EN ADOBO

MODESTO TAPAS BAR AND RESTAURANT > 5257 Shaw Avenue • St. Louis • 314-772-8272 • modestotapas.com

YIELD: 8 APPETIZER SERVINGS (ABOUT 4½ CUPS)

1 pound 4-month-aged
  Manchego cheese
  (see note)

2 tablespoons capers,
  drained and rinsed

½ green bell pepper, seeded
  and chopped

1 small yellow onion, peeled
  and chopped

1 tablespoon chopped
  flat-leaf parsley

½ cup sherry wine vinegar

1 teaspoon sea salt

1 teaspoon chopped garlic

¾ cup fruity extra-virgin
  olive oil

½ teaspoon ground black
  pepper

1 cup pitted manzanilla olives
  (not stuffed), sliced

½ cup roasted red peppers
  (preferably Spanish
  piquillo), drained and
  chopped

Remove rind from cheese; cut cheese into 1-inch cubes.

Combine cheese and remaining ingredients in a large bowl; mix well. Marinate at room temperature for 30 minutes before serving. (Or cover and refrigerate for up to 1 week.)

Note: Manchego is available at many markets that sell imported cheeses. It is firm, but not as hard as Parmesan and with a less assertive flavor.

Per serving:

476 calories

44g fat

83% calories from fat

17g saturated fat

61mg cholesterol

15g protein

5g carbohydrate

1g sugar

0.5g fiber

1,079mg sodium

619mg calcium

89mg potassium

GOAT CHEESE RAREBIT

THE SCHLAFLY TAP ROOM > 2100 Locust Street • St. Louis • 314-241-2337 • schlafly.com

YIELD: 4 SERVINGS (ABOUT ¾ CUP EACH)

1½ cups heavy cream

¼ teaspoon salt

³⁄₈ teaspoon ground black pepper

¾ teaspoon dried tarragon

⅛ teaspoon ground red (cayenne) pepper

⅛ teaspoon Worcestershire sauce

6 ounces goat cheese (chevre), softened

6 ounces cream cheese, softened

2 teaspoons all-purpose flour

Toasted baguette slices

Combine cream, salt, black pepper, tarragon, cayenne and Worcestershire in a medium pot with a heavy bottom. (If you don't have a pot with a heavy bottom, place a pot in a skillet to insulate the cheese mixture from the direct heat.) Cook over low heat just until cream is hot, stirring occasionally.

In the large bowl of an electric mixer, combine goat cheese, cream cheese and flour; beat until flour is incorporated.

Whisk cheeses into hot cream, whisking constantly until mixture is smooth. Cook until heated through, whisking occasionally. Serve warm with toasted bread. (If not serving immediately, keep warm in an uncovered double-boiler over hot water, or cover and place in a 150-degree oven.)

Per serving:

629 calories

61g fat

87% calories from fat

39g saturated fat

203mg cholesterol

14g protein

6g carbohydrate

1g sugar

no fiber

526mg sodium

224mg calcium

200mg potassium

CHICKEN SPRING ROLLS

BUGATTI'S STEAK AND PASTA > Ameristar Casino • St. Charles • 636-940-44471 • ameristar.com/stcharles

YIELD: 4 SPRING ROLLS

1 teaspoon Cajun spice

5 to 6 ounces boneless, skinless chicken breast

1 teaspoon prepared black bean sauce (see note)

½ cup shredded pepper Jack cheese

4 spring roll wrappers (see note)

1 teaspoon chopped cilantro, divided

1 egg yolk, beaten

Vegetable oil, for deep-frying

About ¼ cup sweet chili sauce, for dipping (see note)

Prepare a medium-hot fire in a grill or heat a grill pan. Sprinkle Cajun spice over chicken; grill chicken until cooked through. Let chicken cool, then cut into thin strips.

Mix black bean sauce with shredded cheese; set aside.

Place a spring roll wrapper on the work surface in front of you with one corner pointing down (like a diamond). Stack ¼ of the chicken strips across the diamond, about ⅓ of the way up from the point nearest you. Top with ¼ teaspoon cilantro and ¼ of the cheese mixture.

Moisten the edges of the wrapper with egg yolk. Fold the bottom point of the wrapper up over the filling, then fold the sides toward the center. Roll as tightly as possible without tearing. Press edges gently to seal. Repeat with remaining wrappers and filling.

Heat oil to 350 degrees; fry rolls about 4 minutes, until outside is golden brown and internal temperature reaches 165 degrees. Drain on paper towels; serve with sweet chili dipping sauce.

Note: Spring roll wrappers (approximately 6 inches square), black bean sauce and sweet chili sauce (such as Mae Ploy brand) are available at Asian markets.

Per roll (without chili sauce):

265 calories

12g fat

41% calories from fat

4g saturated fat

90mg cholesterol

16g protein

23g carbohydrate

4g sugar

1g fiber

610mg sodium

130mg calcium

115mg potassium

CHICKEN LIVER MOUSSE

REVIVAL was located on Chouteau Avenue in St. Louis.

YIELD: 12 SERVINGS (ABOUT 2½ CUPS)

1¼ pounds chicken livers

1¼ cups buttermilk

2 shallots, minced (about ⅓ cup), plus more for garnish

1 tablespoon minced garlic

Leaves from 1 sprig fresh rosemary

Leaves from 10 sprigs fresh thyme

¼ cup sherry vinegar

¼ cup heavy (whipping) cream

1 cup (2 sticks) unsalted butter, softened

1 teaspoon salt or to taste

½ teaspoon ground black pepper or to taste

Minced chives, for garnish

Drain livers; place in a bowl and cover with buttermilk. Toss to coat. Cover bowl and refrigerate overnight.

Place livers in a colander over a bowl. Return to refrigerator to drain well, about 20 minutes. Discard buttermilk.

Place a sauté pan over high heat until very hot; add livers and cook, stirring often, until they are thoroughly browned but not cooked through, about 5 minutes. Add shallots and garlic; cook, stirring, until shallots are soft. Add rosemary and thyme; cook about 1 minute. Pour into a bowl and set aside.

Reduce heat slightly; add vinegar to pan and stir to deglaze. Cook until liquid has almost completely evaporated, about 1 minute. Add cream and bring to a boil. Remove from heat and set aside.

Place softened butter in the bowl of a food processor; add livers and purée. Add vinegar-cream reduction, salt and pepper; process to mix thoroughly. Press through a fine strainer. Shape as desired (see tester's note), cover and chill.

Before serving, let come to room temperature; garnish with minced shallots and chives.

Tester's note: After straining mousse, place in serving dish, cover and chill. Or, to form shapes, place in a shallow bowl, cover and chill just until moldable. Press into plastic wrap-lined molds or shape as desired; chill until firm. Be sure to keep mousse well covered to prevent discoloration and dried-out surface area.

Per serving:

223 calories
19.5g fat
79% calories from fat
12g saturated fat
211mg cholesterol
9g protein
3g carbohydrate
0.5g sugar
no fiber
232mg sodium
15mg calcium
125mg potassium

SWEET POTATO SALSA

BLEEDING DEACON PUBLIC HOUSE > 4123 Chippewa Street • St. Louis • 314-772-1813

YIELD: 9 CUPS (ABOUT 18 SERVINGS)

Salt

3 large sweet potatoes, peeled and cut into ½-inch cubes

Vegetable oil

2 large red bell peppers (see note)

4 ears corn, shucked (see note)

½ cup olive oil

⅓ cup lemon juice

3 tablespoons granulated sugar

½ teaspoon Tabasco sauce or to taste

1½ teaspoons dried red pepper flakes

1½ teaspoons ground black pepper

2 (14-ounce) cans black beans, drained and rinsed

1 bunch green onions, sliced into ¼-inch pieces

Tortilla chips, for serving

In a medium pot, bring 1 gallon salted water to a boil. Add diced sweet potatoes. Return to a boil, then cook until potatoes are tender but still firm, about 4 minutes more. Drain potatoes; cover with cold water to stop cooking. Let cool.

Meanwhile, prepare a hot fire in the grill. Lightly oil bell peppers. Place over flames on grill; cook until skin is blackened, turning peppers frequently. Place in a bowl, cover with plastic wrap and allow to cool. Remove skin, stems and seeds; dice peppers into ¼-inch pieces.

Brush corn with vegetable oil; place over flames until kernels are slightly blackened, turning ears frequently. Let cool; scrape kernels into a bowl. (You should have about 2 cups.)

In a large bowl, whisk together olive oil, lemon juice, sugar, Tabasco, pepper flakes, 1 tablespoon salt or to taste and black pepper. Drain cooled sweet potatoes well and add to bowl. Add red peppers and corn. Add black beans and green onions; toss gently to combine.

Cover and chill 1 hour. Serve with tortilla chips.

Note: Prepared roasted red peppers may be substituted; use about 1 cup diced. If no grill is available to roast the corn, substitute 2 cups frozen corn, thawed; sauté in 2 tablespoons olive oil over high heat until kernels begin to brown.

Per ½-cup serving:

138 calories

6g fat

39% calories from fat

1g saturated fat

no cholesterol

3g protein

20g carbohydrate

6g sugar

4g fiber

584mg sodium

29mg calcium

371mg potassium

BRUSCHETTA

HARRY'S RESTAURANT AND BAR > 2144 Market Street • St. Louis • 314-421-6969 • harrysrestaurantandbar.com

YIELD: 12 PIECES (ABOUT 3 SERVINGS)

1 tablespoon plus 2 teaspoons balsamic vinegar

About 1 cup purchased or homemade garlic oil, divided (see note)

2 plum tomatoes, cored and minced

Salt

Ground black pepper

2 large leaves fresh basil, cut into thin strips, plus more for optional garnish

¼ cup jarred roasted red peppers, undrained

1 tablespoon Dijon mustard

1 cup (7½ ounces) soft goat cheese

1 teaspoon dried or chopped fresh chives

1 (8-ounce) loaf French bread (long baguette)

4 ounces fresh mozzarella

Purchased or homemade balsamic glaze (see note)

Prepare tomato topping. In a small bowl, whisk together balsamic vinegar and 1 tablespoon garlic oil. Add tomatoes, and salt and pepper to taste; stir in basil. Set aside for at least 1 hour to allow flavors to blend.

Prepare goat cheese spread. In a blender or food processor, combine roasted red peppers and their liquid with Dijon mustard; process until smooth. Gradually add goat cheese, a spoonful at a time, and salt and pepper to taste. When mixture is smooth and well blended, add chives and pulse one or two times, just to incorporate. Set aside.

Preheat oven to 350 degrees. Slice baguette diagonally to make 12 slices, each about 4 inches long and 2 inches wide. Arrange on a baking sheet; brush with garlic oil. (Refrigerate any leftover homemade garlic oil in a clean jar for up to 10 days.) Bake 5 to 7 minutes, just until slices are golden brown around the edges but still soft in the center. Remove from oven. Increase oven temperature to 375 degrees.

Spread each slice of toasted bread with goat cheese spread.

Use a medium-hole grater to shred the fresh mozzarella. Top each bruschetta with an even layer of shredded mozzarella. Bake just until cheese melts, about 5 minutes.

Use a slotted spoon to top each bruschetta with tomato mixture; drizzle with balsamic glaze. If desired, garnish with basil. Serve immediately.

Notes: To make garlic oil, peel 2 garlic cloves and mash coarsely with the side of a knife. Cook garlic and 1 cup of olive oil or vegetable oil in a small pot over medium-low heat for about 10 minutes, until oil is flavored and fragrant.

To make balsamic glaze, cook about 1 cup balsamic vinegar in a small pan over medium heat until reduced to about ¼ cup (thin syrup consistency). This reduction is excellent as a salad dressing and drizzled over meats, pasta, even pizza. Refrigerate leftovers.

Per piece:

293 calories

25g fat

77% calories from fat

7g saturated fat

16mg cholesterol

7g protein

10g carbohydrate

2g sugar

0.5g fiber

240mg sodium

28mg calcium

35mg potassium

PEAR SALAD WITH CHERRY BALSAMIC VINAIGRETTE

PESTALOZZI PLACE was on Virginia Avenue in St. Louis.

YIELD: 4 SERVINGS

For vinaigrette:

3 ounces dried cherries (about ⅔ cup)

½ cup hot water

2 cloves garlic

¼ cup balsamic vinegar

1 cup extra-virgin olive oil, divided

1 tablespoon Dijon mustard

½ teaspoon salt

½ teaspoon ground white pepper

For pear salad:

6 cups mixed green leaf lettuces

1 cup shredded fontina cheese

2 to 3 green onions (green part only), thinly sliced

½ cup dried cherries

¾ cup Candied Pecans (see recipe)

1 Anjou pear, quartered, cored and sliced

To prepare vinaigrette: Soak cherries in hot water for 15 minutes; pour cherries and liquid into blender container. Add garlic, vinegar and ½ cup olive oil. Process until garlic is finely chopped. Add mustard, salt and pepper, blending after each addition. With blender running, add remaining ½ cup oil in a steady stream. (Makes 2 cups; cover and refrigerate leftovers, and use within a few days.)

To prepare salad: In a bowl, toss lettuce with dressing to taste; divide among 4 serving plates. Sprinkle each salad with cheese, green onions, dried cherries and Candied Pecans, dividing evenly. Arrange pear slices on top of salads.

CANDIED PECANS   YIELD: 4 CUPS

6 cups water

1 pound (4 cups) pecan halves

3 cups vegetable oil, for frying

1 cup powdered sugar, divided

Bring water to a boil in a large pot. Add pecans; boil for 4 to 5 minutes. Pour into a colander and drain thoroughly.

In another deep pot, a wok or an electric deep-fryer, heat oil to 350 degrees. (If using a pot or wok, check temperature with a candy thermometer.)

Scoop about a third of the pecans into a bowl; sprinkle with ⅓ cup powdered sugar, tossing to coat evenly. Scoop sugared pecans into hot oil. Fry until slightly browned, 3 to 4 minutes. Use a slotted spoon to lift nuts from oil onto a baking sheet, arranging nuts in a single layer. (Do not line sheet with paper towels, or pecans will stick.) Repeat with remaining sugar and pecans. Let cool completely.

Note: These pecans will keep for weeks. They make a great addition to many dishes.

Per serving (salad plus ¼ cup dressing):

422 calories
32g fat
68% calories from fat
7.5g saturated fat
31mg cholesterol
10.5g protein
23g carbohydrate
14.5g sugar
5.5g fiber
288mg sodium
221mg calcium
464mg potassium

Candied pecans per ¼-cup serving:

247 calories
21.5g fat
78% calories from fat
2g saturated fat
no cholesterol
2.5g protein
11g carbohydrate
8.5g sugar
2.5g fiber
no sodium
20mg calcium
116mg potassium

29

GRILLED GREEN BEAN AND SMOKED TOMATO SALAD

SQUARE ONE BREWERY > 1727 Park Avenue • St. Louis • 314-231-2537 • squareonebrewery.com

YIELD: 4 SERVINGS

For smoked tomatoes:

1 tablespoon olive oil

1 pinch dried oregano

1 pinch dried thyme

$\frac{1}{8}$ teaspoon California garlic pepper

2 plum tomatoes, quartered lengthwise

For honey-Dijon vinaigrette:

2 tablespoons honey

2 tablespoons rice wine vinegar

2 tablespoons Dijon mustard

1 tablespoon granulated sugar

$\frac{3}{8}$ teaspoon California-style garlic pepper

3 tablespoons extra-virgin olive oil

3 tablespoons vegetable oil

For salad:

Salt

1 pound fresh green beans

Ground black pepper

About 2 teaspoons olive oil

$\frac{1}{2}$ cup thinly sliced red onion

8 ounces gorgonzola cheese, crumbled

To prepare smoked tomatoes: In a small bowl, stir together olive oil, oregano, thyme and garlic pepper; add tomato wedges and toss to coat well.

Place in a smoker over hickory chips and smoke until tomatoes begin to soften. (Tomatoes also can be cooked in a stove-top or oven smoker. Alternately, place tomatoes on a rack inside a pan with damp hickory chips in the bottom. Cover tightly and bake at 350 degrees for 20 minutes or until softened.) Set tomatoes aside.

To prepare vinaigrette: In a blender, combine honey, vinegar, mustard, sugar and garlic pepper; pulse until well mixed. Combine olive oil and vegetable oil in a 1-cup measuring cup with a spout. With blender running, gradually add oil through hole in lid. (Yield: about 10 tablespoons.)

To prepare salad: Prepare a medium-hot fire in the grill (or use a grill pan).

Bring a large pot of salted water to a boil. Add green beans; cook just until crisp-tender. Drain well. Toss with salt and pepper to taste and just enough olive oil to coat lightly. Place beans on a hot grill; leave just long enough to make grill marks and to introduce a grilled flavor. Let beans cool completely.

Toss cooled beans with red onion and $\frac{1}{2}$ cup vinaigrette or to taste. Just before serving, toss with gorgonzola; garnish with smoked tomatoes.

Per serving:

502 calories

38g fat

68% calories from fat

15g saturated fat

51mg cholesterol

15g protein

25g carbohydrate

14g sugar

7g fiber

1,009mg sodium

354mg calcium

345mg potassium

CHOPPED VEGGIE SALAD

GRAFTON'S LANDING BAR AND GRILL was located in Grafton.

YIELD: 4 SERVINGS

For dressing:

¼ cup apple cider vinegar

¼ cup soy sauce

½ cup vegetable oil

1 tablespoon lemon juice

For salad:

1½ hearts of romaine, diced

⅓ cup diced green bell
  pepper (see note)

⅓ cup peeled, seeded, diced
  cucumber

¼ cup diced red onion

⅓ cup diced celery

½ cup diced tomato

¼ cup shredded carrots

⅓ cup sunflower kernels

½ cup grated Parmesan
  cheese

To prepare dressing: Whisk together vinegar, soy sauce, oil and lemon juice. (Makes 1 cup dressing.)

To prepare salad: Toss together romaine, green pepper, cucumber, onion, celery, tomato and carrots. Just before serving, whisk dressing to recombine, then add to taste. Add sunflower kernels and Parmesan; toss to combine.

Note: All diced vegetables should be in ¼-inch pieces.

Per serving:

264 calories

22g fat

75% calories from fat

4g saturated fat

9mg cholesterol

7g protein

9.5g carbohydrate

3g sugar

3g fiber

682mg sodium

147mg calcium

266mg potassium

BAMBINO'S SALAD

BAMBINO'S RESTAURANT AND BAR > 3601 Commerce Drive • Arnold • 636-282-1100

YIELD: 2 LARGE MAIN-DISH SALADS

4 slices prosciutto, chopped or cut into thin strips

3 cups torn romaine lettuce

6 to 7 cups torn iceberg lettuce

4 thin slices red onion

3 to 4 tablespoons diced roasted red peppers

½ cup sliced black olives

2 whole marinated artichoke hearts

6 tablespoons grated Parmesan

¾ cup shredded provolone

Bambino's Dressing (see note)

Pepperoncinis, for garnish

In a small skillet, sauté prosciutto briefly, just until crisp; let cool.

In a large bowl, toss together lettuces, onion, red peppers, olives, artichoke hearts, Parmesan and provolone; add prosciutto. Add dressing to taste; toss well.

Divide between chilled salad plates; garnish with pepperoncinis.

Note: To make the dressing, stir together 1½ to 2 tablespoons chopped fresh basil and 1½ tablespoons olive oil in a small dish; let marinate 10 to 15 minutes. In a bowl, whisk together 2 tablespoons red wine vinegar, 1 teaspoon superfine sugar, 1 pinch salt, cracked black pepper to taste and 1½ teaspoons lemon juice. Slowly whisk in ½ cup vegetable oil. Whisk in marinated basil and oil.

YIELD: ABOUT 14 TABLESPOONS.

Per tablespoon: 83 calories; 9g fat; 0.5g carbohydrate.

Per serving (without dressing):

381 calories

23g fat

54% calories from fat

11g saturated fat

64mg cholesterol

28g protein

15.5g carbohydrate

4g sugar

4g fiber

1,881mg sodium

560mg calcium

371mg potassium

BROCCOLI SLAW

CARDWELL'S AT THE PLAZA > 94 Plaza Frontenac • Frontenac • 314-997-8885 • billcardwell.com

YIELD: 5 SERVINGS

2 or 3 tablespoons golden raisins

1 cup refrigerated coleslaw dressing (see note)

2 tablespoons Dijon mustard

2 tablespoons prepared horseradish

2 tablespoons cider vinegar

1 teaspoon celery salt

1 teaspoon celery seed

1 teaspoon crushed caraway seed (see tester's note)

1 teaspoon dried dill

1 teaspoon garlic powder

½ teaspoon freshly ground white pepper or to taste

1 (16-ounce) bag broccoli slaw mix

2 tablespoons roasted sunflower kernels, plus 1 teaspoon for optional garnish

¼ teaspoon salt or to taste

Sliced green onions, for optional garnish

In a small bowl, cover 2 tablespoons raisins with hot water. Let stand 15 minutes.

In a mixing bowl, combine coleslaw dressing, mustard, horseradish, vinegar, celery salt, celery seed, caraway seed, dill, garlic powder and white pepper; whisk to combine. (Makes about 1⅓ cups. Leftover dressing can be refrigerated up to two weeks.)

Drain raisins. In a large bowl, combine slaw mix, drained raisins, 2 tablespoons sunflower kernels and ½ cup plus 2 tablespoons dressing; toss to mix well. (If making this ahead, wait until just before serving to mix sunflower kernels into slaw.) Season to taste with salt and additional white pepper if desired.

Garnish with green onions. If desired, sprinkle with 1 tablespoon raisins and 1 teaspoon sunflower kernels.

Note: Marzetti's Slaw Dressing provides the best results.

Tester's notes: To crush caraway seed, you will need a mortar and pestle or a small food processor. If you don't have a way to crack the seeds, substitute about ¼ teaspoon ground caraway.

Per serving:

176 calories

10.5g fat

54% calories from fat

1.5g saturated fat

7mg cholesterol

3.5g protein

17g carbohydrate

10g sugar

3g fiber

507mg sodium

60mg calcium

374mg potassium

CREAM OF ZUCCHINI AND CARROT SOUP

GELATO'S ITALIAN ICE CREAM was located in Alton.

YIELD: 8 SERVINGS

4 cups chicken broth

4 medium zucchini, sliced

2 carrots, sliced

1 onion, chopped

1 (8-ounce) package cream
   cheese, softened, divided

1/8 teaspoon salt

1 dash ground pepper

In a large pot, combine broth, zucchini, carrots and onion; bring to a boil. Reduce heat to a simmer, cover and cook 20 minutes or until carrots are tender. With a slotted spoon or strainer, transfer vegetables to a bowl. Remove 1 cup broth from the pot.

Combine about half the vegetables and 4 ounces cream cheese in a blender container; add 1/2 cup broth. Process until puréed. Stir into the broth.

Purée remaining vegetables with remaining 4 ounces cream cheese and 1/2 cup broth; stir into the pot. Add salt and pepper; serve immediately.

Per serving:

134 calories

10g fat

67% calories from fat

6g saturated fat

34g cholesterol

4g protein

7g carbohydrate

4g sugar

2g fiber

622mg sodium

46mg calcium

359mg potassium

CARROT-GINGER SOUP

MINIONS CAFÉ was in Maplewood.

YIELD: 8 (1½-CUP) SERVINGS

½ cup (1 stick) butter

3 to 4 tablespoons vegetable soup base

1 small onion, chopped

1 tablespoon chopped fresh ginger

8 large carrots, peeled and sliced

12 cups water, divided

2¼ cups sour cream, divided

¼ cup milk

In a soup pot, melt butter with soup base over medium-low heat. Add onion and ginger; sauté briefly. Add carrots and 4 cups water; simmer until carrots are soft, 12 to 15 minutes.

Pour mixture through a sieve; return liquid to pot. Place the carrot mixture and 2 cups water in a blender. Blend until smooth; return to pot. Add remaining 6 cups water, and increase heat to medium-high; cook until hot.

Remove from heat. Whisk in 2 cups sour cream until smooth.

In a small bowl, whisk together remaining ¼ cup sour cream and milk.

To serve, ladle hot soup into bowls. To garnish each serving, fill a spoon with some of the sour cream-milk mixture. Holding the spoon barely above the surface, pour the mixture across the soup in a zigzag or other pattern. Serve immediately.

Per serving:

426 calories

18g fat

38% calories from fat

10g saturated fat

57g cholesterol

20g protein

46g carbohydrate

3g sugar

3g fiber

461mg sodium

145mg calcium

386mg potassium

CHEF BOB'S SQUASH SOUP

AGGIE'S CLOSET AND TEA ROOM > 9036 Veterans Memorial Parkway • O'Fallon, Mo. • 636-379-6878

YIELD: ABOUT 10 (1-CUP) SERVINGS

2 acorn squash (3 to 4 pounds)

3 cups apple juice, divided

1 (15-ounce) can pumpkin

1½ teaspoons ground turmeric

1 teaspoon ground nutmeg, plus more for garnish

½ teaspoon salt

¼ teaspoon ground white pepper

¼ cup granulated sugar

3 cups half-and-half, divided

¾ cup sour cream

¼ cup raisins

¼ cup chopped pecans

Fresh mint sprigs

Preheat oven to 400 degrees. Cut acorn squash in half and remove seeds. Pour water into a baking pan to a depth of about ½ inch; arrange squash in pan, cut-side-down. Bake 35 to 40 minutes or until a fork easily pierces skin; let cool.

Scoop cooled pulp from squash; pulse in batches in a food processor, adding enough of the apple juice to make a smooth purée.

In a large mixing bowl, combine puréed squash, pumpkin, turmeric, nutmeg, salt, white pepper and sugar; mix well. Gradually stir in about half of the remaining apple juice and 1½ cups half-and-half, mixing until smooth. Continue adding apple juice and half-and-half, a small amount at a time, until the mixture has the consistency of pea soup. (You may not need all of the juice and half-and-half.)

In a bowl, stir together sour cream, raisins and pecans.

To serve the soup cold, chill at least 1 hour. To serve hot, place in a pan over low heat just until heated through, stirring often. Garnish with a dollop of sour cream mixture, a sprinkle of nutmeg and a mint sprig.

Per serving:

316 calories

14.5g fat

41% calories from fat

8g saturated fat

34mg cholesterol

5g protein

41.5g carbohydrate

17.5g sugar

7g fiber

273mg sodium

163mg calcium

855mg potassium

CREAM OF MUSHROOM SOUP

THE MISSISSIPPI HALF STEP > 420 East Main Street • Grafton • 618-786-2722 • mississippihalfstep.com

YIELD: 8 (1-CUP) SERVINGS

5 tablespoons olive oil

½ cup minced onion

1 tablespoon minced garlic

8 ounces sliced mushrooms

¾ cup sherry

3 cups vegetable stock

2 cups milk

2 cups heavy cream

2 teaspoons dried tarragon

1 teaspoon dried basil

1 teaspoon salt

1 teaspoon cracked black pepper

½ cup (1 stick) butter

½ cup all-purpose flour

Shredded Parmesan cheese, for garnish

Chopped fresh parsley, for garnish

In a very large pot, combine oil and onion; cook over medium-low heat until onion is translucent. Add garlic and mushrooms; cook until soft, about 5 minutes. Add sherry and simmer until the liquid cooks away, about 12 minutes.

Add stock, milk and cream; increase heat and bring to a boil. Stir in tarragon, basil, salt and pepper; boil for 2 minutes.

In another pot, melt butter; whisk in flour, making a roux. Whisk roux into soup and cook until thickened, 6 to 10 minutes. Serve hot, garnished with Parmesan and parsley.

Per serving:

474 calories

44g fat

83% calories from fat

23g saturated fat

118mg cholesterol

5g protein

14g carbohydrate

4.5g sugar

1g fiber

699mg sodium

127mg calcium

274mg potassium

POTATO SOUP

KENRICK'S MEAT MARKET AND CATERING > 4324 Weber Road • St. Louis • 314-631-2440 • kenricks.com

YIELD: 6 SERVINGS (ABOUT 8 CUPS)

1½ pounds medium potatoes

2 slices bacon, diced

½ cup diced yellow onion

1 rib celery, diced

3 cups milk

1 tablespoon chicken base or 1 chicken bouillon cube

¼ teaspoon salt

¼ teaspoon ground pepper

¼ cup (½ stick) butter or margarine

3 tablespoons all-purpose flour

3 sprigs parsley, minced

¾ cup heavy cream

Chopped green onions, for optional garnish

Shredded Colby cheese, for optional garnish

Diced cooked bacon, for optional garnish

Preheat oven to 350 degrees. Scrub potatoes; pierce each a few times with a sharp knife. Bake potatoes until tender, about 50 minutes to 1 hour. When cool enough to handle, peel and cut into ½-inch cubes. Set aside.

In a large heavy pot, sauté bacon, onion and celery over medium-high heat until celery is tender, about 10 minutes. Drain off any bacon grease. Stir in milk, chicken base, salt and pepper; cook over medium-high heat just until very hot, but do not let boil.

Meanwhile, in a heavy pan, melt butter; whisk in flour to make a roux. Cook until mixture bubbles, then cook about 1 minute more. Gradually whisk roux into soup. Continue to cook, stirring constantly, until thick and creamy. Stir in potatoes, parsley and cream. Serve hot, garnished with green onions, cheese and bacon.

Per serving:

384 calories

24g fat

56% calories from fat

11g saturated fat

55mg cholesterol

8g protein

34g carbohydrate

8g sugar

2g fiber

913mg sodium

192mg calcium

615mg potassium

OLD-FASHIONED NAVY BEAN SOUP

MISSOURI ATHLETIC CLUB > 405 Washington Avenue • St. Louis • 314-231-7220 • mac-stl.org

YIELD: ABOUT 14 CUPS

1 pound Great Northern
   beans

1 ham hock

1 tablespoon tomato paste

2 cups diced onion

2 cups diced celery

2 cups diced carrots

1 cup canned diced tomatoes

2 to 3 teaspoons salt or to
   taste

½ teaspoon ground black
   pepper or to taste

Rinse beans; combine with 8 cups water. Soak overnight in the refrigerator.

To make ham stock, combine ham hock and 1 gallon (16 cups) water in a large pot; simmer 2 hours or until the meat releases easily from the bone. Remove ham hock; let cool. Strain stock and refrigerate. When meat is cool, remove from the bone and dice into small cubes; refrigerate.

Transfer beans and their soaking liquid to a large pot; add tomato paste, ham stock, onion, celery, carrots and tomatoes. Bring to a boil over medium-high heat; reduce heat and cook at a low boil for 2 hours, adding water as needed. Add diced ham; cook 30 minutes. Season with salt and pepper to taste.

Per cup:

259 calories

5g fat

17% calories from fat

2g saturated fat

71mg cholesterol

30g protein

23.5g carbohydrate

4g sugar

7g fiber

1,573mg sodium

83mg calcium

725mg potassium

SNACKS AND
STARTERS

SALADS, SOUPS, SIDES AND SAUCES

MAIN DISHES

DESSERTS AND
BAKED GOODS

SOUTHWESTERN CHICKEN SOUP

JACKSONS' > 6655 Manchester Road • St. Louis • 314-645-4904

YIELD: 10 (1-CUP) SERVINGS

2 chicken breast halves

2 tablespoons Cajun spice or to taste, divided

1½ cups diced celery

1½ cups diced onion

1 tablespoon olive oil

⅓ cup sliced black olives

⅓ cup roasted corn kernels

½ cup chopped tomato

¼ cup diced cooked bacon

1½ teaspoons garlic powder

¼ teaspoon dried thyme

Salt

Ground black pepper

4 cups half-and-half

2 cups milk

1 tablespoon chicken base

2 tablespoons water

6 tablespoons butter

6 tablespoons all-purpose flour

Tortilla strips, for garnish (see note)

Provel or Monterey Jack cheese, for garnish

Preheat grill. Rub chicken with about 1 tablespoon Cajun spice. Grill chicken until done. Cut into ½-inch cubes and set aside.

In a large pot, combine celery, onion and olive oil; sauté over medium heat until translucent, about 10 minutes. Add olives, corn, tomato, bacon, remaining 1 tablespoon Cajun spice or to taste, garlic powder, thyme and salt and pepper to taste. Add half-and-half and milk; bring almost to a boil. Dissolve chicken base in water; whisk into pot.

In a small skillet, melt butter over low heat; whisk in flour. Cook 3 or 4 minutes, whisking constantly, until bubbly, making a roux. Gradually whisk into soup to desired consistency. (You may not need all the roux.) Stir in chicken; cook just until hot.

Garnish each serving with tortilla strips and cheese.

Note: To make tortilla strips, cut a flour tortilla into ⅛-inch-wide strips; cut to 1-inch lengths. Fry in hot oil just until golden brown; drain well.

Per serving (without garnishes):

341 calories

24g fat

63% calories from fat

13g saturated fat

88mg cholesterol

16g protein

15g carbohydrate

5g sugar

1g fiber

904mg sodium

190mg calcium

416mg potassium

SOUTH TEXAS TORTILLA SOUP

CANYON CAFÉ > 1701 South Lindbergh Boulevard • Frontenac • 314-872-3443 • canyoncafe.com

YIELD: 12 SERVINGS (ABOUT 1 CUP EACH)

- tablespoon olive oil
- green bell pepper, seeded and diced
- 2 poblano peppers, seeded and diced
- medium onion, diced
- 2 cloves garlic, minced
- 5 fresh corn tortillas, diced
- ½ teaspoons ground cumin
- ¼ teaspoon ground black pepper
- ¼ teaspoon dried oregano
- ½ teaspoons New Mexico chile powder (see note)
- cups strong chicken broth (see note)
- ½ (14-ounce) cans diced tomatoes, undrained
- cup tomato purée
- ⅓ cup chopped cilantro
- pound shredded cooked chicken or chopped seafood, optional
- rushed tortilla chips, crumbled queso fresco (cheese) and/or additional chopped cilantro, for optional garnish

In a large heavy pot, heat oil over medium heat; add peppers, onion and garlic. Cook, stirring often, until onions become translucent, about 4 minutes.

Add corn tortillas and stir until they begin to soften, 3 or 4 minutes. Stir in cumin, black pepper, oregano and chile powder.

Gradually stir in broth, tomatoes and tomato purée. Increase heat. Bring to a boil, stirring often to prevent the tortillas from clumping.

Reduce heat and simmer 20 minutes, stirring often. (Soup may be made ahead to this point and frozen. Reheat, then proceed with the recipe.)

Stir in ⅓ cup chopped cilantro. Taste and adjust seasonings. If desired, stir in chicken or seafood; heat through. Garnish each serving with crushed tortilla chips, queso fresco and/or cilantro.

Notes: Chili powder is a combination of spices, including cumin, that is used to flavor pots of chili. Chile powder is ground dried peppers. The New Mexico chile pepper is a specific variety, and the powdered version is sold in Hispanic markets.

To make "strong" chicken broth, make your own and boil it until reduced by half. For a quicker version, used canned broth and add about 1 to 2 tablespoons chicken base, dissolved in a little water.

Per serving:

86 calories

2.5g fat

87% calories from fat

0.5g saturated fat

4mg cholesterol

3g protein

13g carbohydrate

4g sugar

3g fiber

1,123mg sodium

27mg calcium

225mg potassium

LOBSTER BISQUE

BRIO TUSCAN GRILLE > 1601 South Lindbergh Boulevard • Frontenac • 314-432-4410 • brioitalian.com

YIELD: ABOUT 8 (1-CUP) SERVINGS

¼ cup (½ stick) unsalted butter

½ cup olive oil, plus more for garnish

1 tablespoon chopped garlic

¼ cup chopped yellow onion

3 tablespoons all-purpose flour

½ cup tomato paste

¾ cup sweet sherry

3½ cups lobster stock (see note)

2 cups heavy cream

¼ teaspoon ground red (cayenne) pepper

Salt

Ground black pepper

6 ounces cooked lobster meat or shrimp, diced

2 tablespoons chopped parsley

In a large, heavy pot, melt butter with ½ cup oil; add garlic and onion and sauté for 2 minutes. Whisk in flour; cook until light brown, about 3 minutes. Whisk in tomato paste and simmer for 2 minutes. Add sherry; cook about 3 minutes. Stir in lobster stock; simmer about 20 minutes. Strain through mesh strainer, discarding solids. Stir heavy cream into liquid; add cayenne and salt and black pepper to taste. Stir in cooked shrimp or lobster.

Garnish each serving with a drizzle of olive oil and a pinch of chopped parsley.

Note: For lobster stock, stir lobster base into warm water as directed on jar; stir until completely dissolved.

Per serving:

454 calories

42g fat

83% calories from fat

19g saturated fat

113mg cholesterol

7g protein

12g carbohydrate

3g sugar

1g fiber

847mg sodium

70mg calcium

334mg potassium

LOBSTER MAC AND CHEESE

LUCAS PARK GRILLE > 1234 Washington Avenue • St. Louis • 314-241-7770 • lucasparkgrille.com

YIELD: 8 SIDE-DISH SERVINGS

1 pound elbow macaroni

3 tablespoons all-purpose flour

3 tablespoons butter, melted

3¼ cups whole milk

8 ounces mascarpone cheese

3 to 4 tablespoons roasted garlic (see note)

10 ounces mild Cheddar cheese or more to taste, shredded

8 ounces cooked lobster claw and knuckle meat, chopped

Salt

Ground pepper

Grated Parmesan, for garnish

Cook macaroni until al dente; drain and keep warm.

In a small bowl, make a roux by whisking flour into melted butter. Set aside.

In a large pot or Dutch oven, combine milk, mascarpone and roasted garlic. Whisk over medium heat until smooth and steaming; whisk in roux and cook until thickened.

Add Cheddar to simmering sauce and whisk until incorporated. Fold in lobster. Add macaroni and simmer 2 minutes more or until heated through, stirring constantly. Add salt and pepper to taste. Transfer to a serving dish and sprinkle with Parmesan.

Chef's note: For a great fried mac-and-cheese appetizer, refrigerate leftovers overnight. Use an ice cream scoop to form into 2-inch balls; freeze. Just before serving, roll balls in flour seasoned with salt and pepper. Dip into beaten egg, then roll in panko bread crumbs. Deep-fry at 350 degrees for about 3 minutes or until golden brown.

Note: To roast garlic, slice the top ¼ inch off a whole, unpeeled bulb of garlic, exposing the pulp of each clove. Place in a shallow baking dish and drizzle with 1 to 2 teaspoons olive oil (more if you want extra garlic-flavored oil to use in other dishes). Cover with foil and bake in a preheated 325-degree oven for 20 minutes or until pulp is soft, fragrant and golden brown. Cool. Squeeze pulp from bulb and mash. For convenience, roast several bulbs at a time, squeeze the roasted pulp into small plastic containers, and freeze for future use.

Per serving:

626 calories

34g fat

49% calories from fat

20g saturated fat

120mg cholesterol

30g protein

50g carbohydrate

7g sugar

2g fiber

340mg sodium

445mg calcium

360mg potassium

CORN SOUFFLÉ

HIGHWAY 61 ROADHOUSE > 34 South Old Orchard Avenue • Webster Groves • 314-968-0061 • hwy61roadhouse.com

YIELD: 8 SERVINGS

1 (15-ounce) can whole-kernel corn, drained

1 (15-ounce) can cream-style corn

2¼ cups (about 10 ounces) corn muffin mix

½ cup vegetable oil

2 eggs, lightly beaten

¾ cup sour cream

2¼ ounces (about ⅔ cup) shredded Cheddar cheese

Honey Butter (1 stick softened butter beaten with ¼ cup honey), for garnish

Preheat the oven to 350 degrees. Coat a 9-by-13-inch baking pan with non-stick cooking spray; set aside.

In a large bowl, combine all ingredients; mix well. Pour mixture into prepared pan and bake 40 to 45 minutes or until browned around the edges and set in the center. Serve hot with Honey Butter.

Note: At Highway 61 Roadhouse, this corn soufflé is served as a side dish. Individual servings are baked in 5- or 6-inch pie pans for 25 minutes.

Per serving:
578 calories
38g fat
59% calories from fat
15g saturated fat
102mg cholesterol
9g protein
50g carbohydrate
20g sugar
4g fiber
770mg sodium
115mg calcium
176mg potassium

CRESCENT CITY CREAMED SPINACH

RUTH'S CHRIS STEAK HOUSE > 1 N. Brentwood Boulevard • Clayton • 314-783-9900 **/** 315 Chestnut Street • St. Louis • 314-259-3200 • ruthschris.com

YIELD: 4 SERVINGS

½ cup (1 stick) plus
  2 tablespoons butter,
  divided

¼ cup all-purpose flour

2 tablespoons chopped onion

1 small bay leaf

¼ teaspoon salt

2 cups milk or half-and-half

1 pound fresh spinach,
  washed

Salt

Freshly ground black pepper

In a small saucepan, melt ½ cup butter over medium heat until foamy. Set aside remaining 2 tablespoons butter at room temperature.

Add flour to melted butter; cook and stir until light brown. Add onion, bay leaf and salt, then whisk in milk. Cook, stirring, until mixture comes to a boil and thickens. Reduce heat and cook 5 minutes. Pass through a fine strainer, discarding solids. (The sauce will be thick.) Keep sauce warm until serving time.

Bring a large pot of water to a boil. Add spinach; cook for 1 minute. Remove spinach; immediately immerse in ice water to stop cooking. Drain, then squeeze spinach dry. Chop finely or purée in a food processor; set aside.

Just before serving, combine sauce and spinach in a saucepan. Rewarm spinach over low heat, stirring often, about 5 minutes. Season to taste with salt and pepper; stir in softened butter.

Per serving:
339 calories
27g fat
72% calories from fat
17g saturated fat
72mg cholesterol
8g protein
16g carbohydrate
6g sugar
3g fiber
287mg sodium
259mg calcium
830mg potassium

SNACKS AND STARTERS

SALADS, SOUPS, SIDES AND SAUCES

MAIN DISHES

DESSERTS AND BAKED GOODS

61

VANILLA SWEET POTATOES

SUNSET 44 BISTRO > 118 West Adams Avenue • Kirkwood, 314-965-6644 • sunset44.com

YIELD: 12 SERVINGS

1¼ cups 40 percent ("gourmet") whipping cream

2 whole vanilla beans

3 or 4 Japanese white sweet potatoes (about 2¾ pounds) or regular sweet potatoes

½ cup (1 stick) unsalted butter

Place cream in a heavy pot. Split vanilla beans lengthwise and gently scrape pulp and seeds into cream; add pods and bring just to a boil. Turn off heat and allow to steep at least 15 minutes.

Peel sweet potatoes, cut into chunks and immediately place in a pot with enough water to cover. Bring to a boil over high heat, then reduce heat slightly and cook potatoes until fork-tender. Drain potatoes and press through a ricer (or use a potato masher).

Strain cream. Return cream to pan. Add butter; heat to scalding (small bubbles will form around the edge of the liquid). Stir in potatoes. Serve hot.

Per serving:

217 calories

17g fat

71% calories from fat

11g saturated fat

55mg cholesterol

2g protein

14g carbohydrate

4g sugar

2g fiber

35mg sodium

43mg calcium

320mg potassium

RED BEANS AND RICE

BLUEBERRY HILL > 6504 Delmar Boulevard • University City • 314-727-4444 • BlueberryHill.com

YIELD: 4 TO 6 SERVINGS

2 cups chopped onion

1 green bell pepper, cut into 1-inch pieces

½ rib celery with leaves, chopped

1 cup chopped tomato

1 tablespoon plus 1 teaspoon minced garlic

3 (15- to 16-ounce) cans kidney beans, drained

1 cup water

1 bay leaf

1 tablespoon dried basil

2 teaspoons dried thyme

1 teaspoon salt

1 teaspoon ground black pepper

1½ teaspoons Tabasco sauce or to taste

Hot cooked white or brown rice (see note)

Combine onion, green pepper, celery, tomato, garlic, beans, water, bay leaf, basil, thyme, salt, pepper and Tabasco sauce in a large pot. Bring to a boil, then reduce heat to a simmer. Cook about 30 minutes or until vegetables are tender, stirring occasionally. Remove bay leaf; serve bean mixture over hot rice.

Note: Blueberry Hill serves the beans over seasoned rice. Many varieties of rice mixes are available in local supermarkets, such as vegetable and onion-garlic.

Per serving (based on 6 servings, with ½ cup plain white rice):

334 calories

2g fat

5% calories from fat

0.5 saturated fat

no cholesterol

15g protein

64g carbohydrate

8g sugar

12g fiber

1,076mg sodium

134mg calcium

799mg potassium

TANGY PIT BEANS

17TH STREET BAR AND GRILL > 1711 West Highway 50 • O'Fallon, Ill. • 618-622-1717 • 17thstreetbarbecue.com

YIELD: 14 CUPS

2 tablespoons prepared
    yellow mustard

2⅓ cups ketchup

1 cup diced onion

1 green or red bell pepper,
    seeded and diced

1½ cups packed brown sugar

½ cup sorghum or honey

1 to 1½ tablespoons Magic
    Dust seasoning blend
    (see note)

1 (28-ounce) can pork and
    beans

1 (15- to 16-ounce) can chili-
    seasoned beans

1 (16-ounce) can large red
    kidney beans, drained and
    rinsed

1 (15- to 16-ounce) can butter
    beans, drained and rinsed

1 (15- to 16-ounce) can other
    beans of your choice,
    drained and rinsed

4 to 5 slices cooked bacon
    or a small amount of
    barbecued meat (such as
    pulled pork)

Preheat the oven to 350 degrees. In a large bowl, mix mustard, ketchup, onion, bell pepper, brown sugar, sorghum or honey and Magic Dust; stir until no lumps of brown sugar remain. Fold in beans, mixing gently.

Pour into a 9-by-13-inch baking dish that is at least 2¾ inches deep. (A shallower dish will overflow in the oven.) Distribute meat over beans; cover with foil. Bake 45 minutes, then remove foil and bake 15 minutes or until bubbly. (Leftover beans reheat well and may be frozen.)

Note: To make Magic Dust seasoning, finely grind 1½ teaspoons kosher salt with a mortar and pestle or in a small bowl with the back of a spoon. Combine with 1 tablespoon paprika, 1½ teaspoons granulated sugar, from ¾ to 1½ teaspoons dry mustard, 1½ teaspoons chili powder, 1½ teaspoons ground cumin, from ¾ to 1½ teaspoons ground black pepper, 1½ teaspoons garlic powder and ¾ teaspoon ground red (cayenne) pepper. Stir well. Store in an airtight container.
YIELD: ABOUT ¼ CUP.

Per teaspoon: 8 calories; no fat; 0.5g protein; 1.5g carbohydrate; 0.5g sugar; 0.5g fiber; 244mg sodium; 6mg calcium; 26mg potassium.

Per (1-cup) serving:

374 calories

2g fat

5% calories from fat

0.5g saturated fat

6mg cholesterol

12g protein

77g carbohydrate

47g sugar

10g fiber

1,286mg sodium

117mg calcium

911mg potassium

BRANDY PEPPERCORN SAUCE

CITIZEN KANE'S STEAKHOUSE > 133 West Clinton Place • Kirkwood • 314-965-9005 • citizenkanes.com

YIELD: ABOUT 1¾ CUPS

SNACKS AND
STARTERS

SALADS, SOUPS, SIDES AND SAUCES

MAIN DISHES

DESSERTS AND
BAKED GOODS

2 tablespoon plus 1 teaspoon olive oil

2 teaspoons minced garlic

1 large shallot, chopped (about ½ cup)

¾ teaspoon dried thyme leaves

1 small bay leaf

1½ teaspoons Worcestershire sauce

1½ teaspoons beef base

3 tablespoons brandy

¾ cup plus 2 tablespoons whole milk

½ cup (40 percent) heavy cream, divided

⅓ cup half-and-half, divided

4 teaspoons cornstarch

2 tablespoons plus ½ teaspoon Dijon mustard

2½ teaspoons cracked black peppercorns, plus additional for garnish

In a large pot, heat oil over medium heat. Add garlic, shallot, thyme and bay leaf; cook until shallot is tender, about 6 minutes, stirring often. (Do not allow garlic to scorch.)

Add Worcestershire, beef base and brandy; simmer about 5 minutes or until mixture is syrupy. Stir in milk and cook until hot. Pour through a fine strainer into a clean pot; discard solids.

In a small dish, combine about 2 tablespoons cream, 2 tablespoons half-and-half and cornstarch; whisk together and set aside.

Add remaining cream and half-and-half to strained liquid. Whisk cornstarch mixture again, and whisk into sauce. Place over medium heat; cook, whisking constantly, until thickened. If necessary, strain again through a fine strainer. Whisk in mustard and cracked peppercorns; simmer until heated through. Just before serving, garnish with additional cracked peppercorns.

Note: Serve over filets, as pictured, or other steaks, scallops, salmon, vegetables or pork.

Per (¼-cup) serving:

171 calories

13g fat

68% calories from fat

6g saturated fat

31mg cholesterol

2g protein

8g carbohydrate

2g sugar

no fiber

150mg sodium

69mg calcium

125mg potassium

SNACKS AND
STARTERS

SALADS, SOUPS,
SIDES AND SAUCES

MAIN DISHES

DESSERTS AND
BAKED GOODS

STIR-FRIED SPICY EGGPLANT

P.F. CHANG'S CHINA BISTRO > 25 The Boulevard • Richmond Heights • 314-862-2624 **/** 1295 Chesterfield Pkwy East • Chesterfield • 636-532-0215 • pfchangs.com

YIELD: 1 ENTREE OR 2 SIDE-DISH SERVINGS

1 tablespoon granulated
  sugar

2 tablespoons oyster sauce
  (vegetarian or regular)

2 tablespoons light soy sauce

4 tablespoons water, divided

1 tablespoon white vinegar

1 teaspoon chile paste
  (such as sambal oleck)

½ teaspoon bean sauce
  (such as Koon Chun brand)

½ teaspoon toasted sesame
  oil

1 pound eggplant, peeled

Canola oil, for deep-frying

1 teaspoon minced garlic

1 tablespoon cornstarch

In a small bowl, stir together sugar, oyster sauce, soy sauce, 2 tablespoons water, vinegar, chile paste, bean sauce and sesame oil; mix well.

Cut eggplant into 1-inch cubes. Pour enough oil for deep-frying into a wok; heat to 350 degrees. Add eggplant; fry until slightly softened, 3 or 4 minutes. Remove eggplant with a slotted spoon or skimmer; drain well on paper towels.

Transfer about ½ teaspoon of the oil from the wok to a small pan; place over medium-high heat. Stir in garlic, then add sauce mixture. Bring to a simmer, stirring frequently.

Stir in eggplant. Dissolve cornstarch in remaining 2 tablespoons water; gradually stir into eggplant mixture. Cook until sauce is translucent. Serve immediately.

Per entree serving:

248 calories

16g fat

58% calories from fat

3g saturated fat

no cholesterol

2g protein

24g carbohydrate

11g sugar

6g fiber

1,428mg sodium

27mg calcium

468mg potassium

SPINACH AND GRUYÈRE QUICHE

THE LONDON TEA ROOM > 1520 Washington Avenue • St. Louis • 314-241-6556 • thelondontearoom.com

YIELD: 8 TO 10 SERVINGS

2½ cups all purpose flour

Salt

1 cup (2 sticks) cold butter, cut into cubes

4 to 5 tablespoons ice water

4 eggs

1 cup whole milk

1 cup heavy cream

⅛ teaspoon ground red (cayenne) pepper

2½ ounces prewashed baby spinach (3 to 4 cups)

4 ounces shredded Gruyère cheese (about 1 cup)

Preheat oven to 425 degrees. Grease the bottom and sides of a 9-inch springform pan.

In the work bowl of a food processor, combine flour, a pinch of salt and butter. Pulse until mixture resembles bread crumbs. Gradually add ice water, pulsing just until the mixture forms a dough. Do not overprocess.

Press dough into prepared pan, making sure that dough covers the sides of the pan all the way to the top. Bake 12 to 14 minutes. (Crust will be about half baked. Crust might shrink slightly from the top edge of the pan.) Place crust on a cooling rack; reduce oven temperature to 350 degrees.

In a medium bowl, beat eggs thoroughly with a whisk; add milk, cream, cayenne and a pinch of salt. Whisk until completely blended.

Arrange spinach in pastry shell; sprinkle Gruyère over spinach. Carefully pour egg mixture over the top. Place the pan in the oven on a sheet of foil with the edges pulled up slightly. Bake 1 hour, until lightly golden brown. If the filling still jiggles slightly after 1 hour, bake another 10 minutes or until set. Cut into wedges and serve.

Per serving (based on 10):

456 calories

34g fat

67% calories from fat

20.5g saturated fat

181mg cholesterol

11g protein

26.5g carbohydrate

1.5g sugar

1g fiber

100mg sodium

184mg calcium

128mg potassium

ARTICHOKE QUICHE

MAGPIE'S > 903 South Main Street • St. Charles • 636-947-3883 • magpiesstcharles.com

YIELD: 6 SERVINGS

Pastry for 9-inch deep-dish
pie

1¼ cups shredded Monterey
Jack cheese

1 tablespoon butter

1 tablespoon olive oil

1 large clove garlic, finely
minced

1 cup coarsely chopped
canned (not marinated)
artichoke hearts, drained

½ cup grated Parmesan
cheese

3 eggs

2 cups half-and-half

½ teaspoon salt

¼ teaspoon ground black
pepper or to taste

Preheat oven to 350 degrees. Line a 9-inch deep-dish pie plate with pastry; flute edges. Sprinkle Monterey Jack cheese in an even layer over bottom of pie shell.

Melt butter with oil in a medium skillet over medium heat. Add garlic; cook, stirring for 30 seconds. Add artichokes; sauté until all liquid from artichokes has evaporated, about 5 minutes.

Scatter sautéed artichokes over Monterey Jack cheese in pie shell; sprinkle evenly with Parmesan.

In a medium bowl, beat eggs with half-and-half; stir in salt and pepper. Slowly pour egg mixture into pie shell. Bake on bottom shelf of oven until top puffs and turns golden brown, about 50 to 60 minutes. Let cool 30 minutes before slicing.

Per serving:

432 calories

32g fat

67% calories from fat

16g saturated fat

175mg cholesterol

16g protein

20g carbohydrate

0.5g sugar

no fiber

686mg sodium

349mg calcium

168mg potassium

NOODLE-LESS LASAGNA

SQWIRES > 1415 South 18th Street • St. Louis • 314-865-3522 • sqwires.com

YIELD: 6 SERVINGS

1 pound carrots, peeled

1 (¾-pound) eggplant, ends trimmed

1¼ pounds zucchini, ends trimmed

1 pound yellow squash, ends trimmed

1 pound red onion, peeled

About 10 teaspoons olive oil, divided

1¼ teaspoons salt, divided

1¼ teaspoons ground black pepper, divided

4 cups fresh tomato sauce, divided (see note)

12 ounces chevre (goat cheese), divided

8 ounces grated Parmesan, divided

If using a grill, prepare a medium-hot fire.

Slice carrots, eggplant, zucchini and yellow squash ⅛ inch thick on the diagonal. Slice onion ⅛ inch thick. Place each vegetable in a separate bowl; drizzle each with about 2 teaspoons olive oil, just enough to coat lightly. Sprinkle vegetables in each bowl with ¼ teaspoon salt and ¼ teaspoon pepper. Toss to coat.

Grill vegetables until cooked through and some pieces have charred edges or are slightly browned.

(Alternately, place each vegetable on a baking sheet and broil until vegetables start to brown, 10 to 18 minutes.)

Let vegetables cool.

Preheat the oven to 300 degrees. Coat the bottom of a 9-by-13-inch baking pan with 1 cup tomato sauce. Layer with ¼ of the zucchini, then ¼ of the eggplant, ¼ of the yellow squash, ¼ of the carrots and ¼ of the onions. Top with 3 ounces chevre and 2 ounces Parmesan. Repeat layers three times, ending with cheeses.

Bake 45 minutes. If top has browned after 30 minutes, cover with foil to prevent overbrowning during the last 15 minutes of baking time.

Note: To make fresh tomato sauce, scald and peel tomatoes, cut in about 1-inch chunks and cook for about 30 minutes, seasoning to taste. If using a canned product, make sure it has chunks of tomatoes, such as stewed or diced tomatoes.

Per serving:

551 calories

31g fat

51% calories from fat

16g saturated fat

59mg cholesterol

31g protein

37g carbohydrate

18g sugar

9g fiber

1,350mg sodium

590mg calcium

1,509mg potassium

BROCCOLI LASAGNA

MISS AIMEE B'S TEA ROOM > 837 First Capitol Drive • St. Charles • 636-946-4202 • missaimeeb.com

YIELD: 12 SERVINGS

24 ounces cottage cheese

3 eggs

1 tablespoon chopped fresh parsley

¾ cup grated Parmesan, divided

2 (1-pound) bags frozen broccoli spears, thawed

1 teaspoon garlic powder

15 lasagna noodles, cooked

24 ounces shredded Monterey Jack cheese, divided

2 cups shredded mozzarella, divided

12 slices bacon, cooked crisp and chopped, for garnish

Preheat oven to 350 degrees. Coat a 10-by-15-by-3-inch glass baking pan with nonstick cooking spray.

In a medium bowl, stir together cottage cheese, eggs, parsley and ½ cup Parmesan; set aside.

Squeeze broccoli to remove excess moisture; toss with garlic powder.

Line the baking pan with 5 lasagna noodles, top with ⅓ of the cottage cheese mixture, then ⅓ of the broccoli and ⅓ of the Monterey Jack. Sprinkle with ½ cup mozzarella. Repeat layers twice, topping with the remaining 1 cup mozzarella and then the reserved ¼ cup Parmesan.

Cover with foil, making sure it does not rest on the cheese. (If dish is very full, place the dish on a large sheet of foil, and mold the foil into shape by pressing it up the sides of the pan. Lift the pan and place on the counter. Invert the foil over the lasagna to make a domed "lid.")

Bake 45 minutes, then remove foil and bake 10 minutes. Garnish each serving with chopped bacon.

Per serving:
492 calories
28g fat
51% calories from fat
16g saturated fat
138mg cholesterol
35g protein
25g carbohydrate
5g sugar
3g fiber
878mg sodium
703mg calcium
242mg potassium

SNACKS AND
STARTERS

SALADS, SOUPS,
SIDES AND SAUCES

MAIN DISHES

DESSERTS AND
BAKED GOODS

PASTA WITH BROCCOLI

MADISON'S CAFE > 2974 Highway K • O'Fallon, Mo. • 636-978-7355 • madisonsofallon.com

YIELD: 2 OR 3 SERVINGS

8 ounces cavatelli pasta

12 frozen or fresh broccoli florets (2 to 3 cups)

3 cups half-and-half

6 tablespoons (¾ stick) butter or margarine

1½ cups thinly sliced fresh mushrooms

1 teaspoon minced garlic

⅛ teaspoon ground red (cayenne) pepper

⅛ teaspoon ground white pepper

½ cup spicy marinara sauce or regular marinara mixed with a pinch of cayenne pepper

1 to 1½ cups freshly grated Parmesan cheese

Salt

In a large pot, cook pasta just until tender; drain well. Return to pot. Meanwhile, if using fresh broccoli, steam until tender-crisp; drain. (Frozen broccoli does not need to be precooked.)

Add broccoli, half-and-half, butter, mushrooms, garlic, cayenne, white pepper and marinara to pasta; stir to combine.

Bring to a boil, stirring often. Boil for about 1 minute, then add Parmesan, reduce heat to medium and cook until sauce thickens to desired consistency. Add salt to taste. (If sauce thickens too much, stir in a little more half-and-half.)

Per serving (based on 3):

768 calories

64g fat

75% calories from fat

39g saturated fat

186mg cholesterol

27g protein

23g carbohydrate

5g sugar

3.5g fiber

910mg sodium

749mg calcium

850mg potassium

PASTA PORTOBELLO A LA LILLY

CANDICCI'S ITALIAN GRILLE > 100 Holloway Road • Ballwin • 636-220-8989 • candiccis.net

YIELD: 1 LARGE SERVING

6 ounces uncooked fettuccine or pasta of your choice

2 tablespoons butter

¼ cup extra-virgin olive oil

2 to 4 large cloves garlic, minced

½ cup sliced roasted red bell peppers

2 cups sliced portobello mushrooms

1 boneless, skinless chicken breast half, grilled or baked, then diced

1 plum tomato, chopped

Salt

Ground black pepper

Cook pasta al dente; drain and keep warm.

In a large skillet, melt butter with oil over medium heat. Add garlic; sauté until beginning to soften, about 1 minute. Add peppers and mushrooms; cook briefly, stirring, until mushrooms are about half cooked. Add chicken and pasta; cook until warmed through. Toss in the tomatoes, season to taste with salt and pepper, and serve immediately.

Per serving:

1,528 calories

84.5g fat

50% calories from fat

24g saturated fat

123mg cholesterol

52g protein

140g carbohydrate

14g sugar

9g fiber

80mg sodium

75mg calcium

1,215mg potassium

PASTA PRIMAVERA

TONY'S > 410 South Broadway • St. Louis • 314-231-7007

YIELD: 3 SERVINGS

1 pound capellini (angel hair pasta)

2½ cups finely minced fresh vegetables (such as asparagus, broccoli, cauliflower, zucchini, mushrooms)

6 tablespoons (¾ stick) butter

2 plum tomatoes, diced

¼ teaspoon dried red pepper flakes or to taste

Salt

Freshly ground black pepper

Put enough water to cook 1 pound of pasta into a large pot; bring to a boil. Add vegetables and cook about 2 minutes. Add pasta and cook until almost done.

Ladle about 1½ cups of the cooking liquid into a measuring cup and set aside. Drain pasta and vegetables, discarding remaining liquid.

In the empty pot, combine butter, tomatoes and red pepper flakes; stir together over medium-high heat until butter melts. Stir in reserved liquid. Return cooked pasta and vegetables to the pot, season with salt and pepper to taste and toss to mix well. Serve immediately.

Per serving:

785 calories

25g fat

29% calories from fat

15g saturated fat

60mg cholesterol

23g protein

118g carbohydrate

9g sugar

7g fiber

30mg sodium

60mg calcium

RIGATONI ALL'AMATRICIANA

ROBERTO'S TRATTORIA > 145 Concord Plaza • St. Louis County • 314-842-9998 • robertostrattoriastl.com

YIELD: 2 SERVINGS

6 tablespoons olive oil

½ pound pancetta, sliced about ¼ inch thick (see note)

⅓ cup chopped white onion

2 cloves garlic, minced

¼ cup white wine

1 (28-ounce) can whole peeled tomatoes

Salt

Ground black pepper

¼ teaspoon red pepper flakes or to taste

8 to 10 leaves fresh basil, chopped

3 to 6 tablespoons butter, optional

½ pound rigatoni, cooked and drained

Grated Parmesan or Romano cheese, for garnish

In a heavy, deep skillet, heat olive oil over medium heat.

Chop pancetta into ¼-inch cubes; add to olive oil and cook 1 to 2 minutes. Stir in onion and garlic; cook 1 to 2 minutes, being careful not to scorch garlic. Stir in wine and cook for another minute or two.

Meanwhile, drain tomatoes, reserving juice. Chop tomatoes finely. Add tomatoes and juice to skillet; stir in salt and black pepper to taste and red pepper flakes. Bring to a simmer, then reduce heat and let simmer uncovered about 20 minutes, until liquid is reduced by at least half.

Stir in basil. If desired, add butter to thicken and flavor the sauce. Toss with hot pasta. Garnish with a sprinkling of cheese.

Note: Pancetta is referred to as Italian bacon, but it is not smoked, unlike American bacon. The closest substitute is prosciutto, available in most large grocery stores.

Per serving:

1,149 calories
54.5g fat
43% calories from fat
10g saturated fat
89mg cholesterol
51.5g protein
108g carbohydrate
18g sugar
7g fiber
3,829mg sodium
39mg calcium
250mg potassium

BOW-TIE JACK PASTA

THE HAWTHORNE INN > 123 Front Street • Labadie • 636-451-0004

YIELD: 4 SERVINGS

3 cups half-and-half

3 tablespoons margarine or butter

1 tablespoon freshly minced garlic

1 pound shrimp, peeled and deveined

8 ounces grilled chicken, cut into strips

1/3 cup sun-dried tomatoes, cut into thin strips

4 ounces gorgonzola cheese, crumbled (about 1 cup)

1 pound bow-tie pasta, cooked and drained

1 cup freshly grated Parmesan cheese

1/4 pound bacon, cooked crisp and cut into bite-size pieces

Salt

Freshly ground black pepper

Sliced green onions, for garnish

In a large saucepan or Dutch oven, combine half-and-half, margarine, garlic, shrimp, grilled chicken and sun-dried tomatoes. Cook over high heat until cream reaches a boil.

Stir in gorgonzola and cooked pasta. Continue to cook until cream begins to bubble again. Gradually stir in Parmesan; cook to desired consistency. (Sauce will thicken with the addition of Parmesan.) Stir in bacon. Add salt and pepper to taste; garnish with green onions.

Per serving:

1,185 calories

53.5g fat

41% calories from fat

26g saturated fat

340g cholesterol

79g protein

97g carbohydrate

7g sugar

5g fiber

1,578mg sodium

797mg calcium

918mg potassium

SHRIMP PASTA WITH VODKA SAUCE

MANGIA ITALIANO > 3145 South Grand Boulevard • St. Louis • 314-664-8585 • dineatmangia.com

YIELD: 4 SERVINGS

6 ounces pancetta, diced

1 yellow onion, diced

6 tablespoons vodka

1 cup heavy (whipping) cream

1 cup fresh tomato sauce

½ cup grated Pecorino Romano cheese

Salt

Ground black pepper

2 tablespoons olive oil

20 jumbo shrimp

1¼ pounds fresh conchiglie pasta (ridged shells; see note)

In a skillet over low heat, cook pancetta until crispy; add onion and cook until translucent. When most of the liquid has evaporated, stand back and add vodka to deglaze the pan. Cook long enough to burn off the alcohol, about 3 minutes, then add cream and tomato sauce. Continue cooking until reduced by half. Remove from heat and stir in cheese. Add salt and pepper to taste. Set aside and keep warm.

Place a large skillet over medium heat; when hot, add olive oil and shrimp. Cook just until shrimp turn pink; stir into sauce.

Meanwhile, bring a large pot of salted water to a boil. When sauce and shrimp are done, add fresh pasta to boiling water. Cook just until done, about 1 to 3 minutes. Drain well. Add to sauce and shrimp and toss well.

Variation: Instead of shrimp, you can use about 2 chicken breast halves, grilled and sliced.

Note: You can substitute 12 ounces dried pasta.

Per serving:

967 calories

49g fat

46% calories from fat

23g saturated fat

278mg cholesterol

37g protein

87g carbohydrate

4g sugar

7g fiber

1,190mg sodium

261mg calcium

620mg potassium

ALFREDO GRILL PASTA

ALFREDO GRILL was in St. Charles.

YIELD: 2 SERVINGS

6 ounces rotini pasta

1 (6-ounce) boneless chicken breast half

3 tablespoons butter, melted

¼ cup seasoned dry bread crumbs

1¼ cups half-and-half or more as needed

¼ teaspoon salt

⅛ teaspoon ground black pepper or to taste

¼ teaspoon dried red pepper flakes

4 ounces shredded Cheddar cheese (about 1½ cups)

½ cup string provel cheese, plus extra for optional garnish

⅔ cup grated Parmesan cheese

Chopped fresh parsley, for garnish

Cook pasta according to package directions; drain well and set aside.

Place chicken between two sheets of plastic wrap. With a meat pounder or rolling pin, pound chicken to about ½ inch thick.

Place melted butter in a shallow bowl. Place bread crumbs in another shallow bowl. Dip chicken in butter, coating completely, then coat with bread crumbs. Cook under a hot broiler until firm. Cut into ¾-inch cubes; set aside.

In a large pot, combine half-and-half, salt, black pepper and red pepper flakes; add chicken and bring to a boil. Stir in cheeses, then fold in cooked pasta; heat through. If sauce is too thick, add a bit more half-and-half. Garnish with additional provel, if desired, and parsley.

Per serving:

1,313 calories

74.5g fat

51% calories from fat

45g saturated fat

279mg cholesterol

77.5g protein

83g carbohydrate

5g sugar

3.5g fiber

1,741mg sodium

1,174mg calcium

714mg potassium

SNACKS AND
STARTERS

SALADS, SOUPS,
SIDES AND SAUCES

MAIN DISHES

DESSERTS AND
BAKED GOODS

CHICKEN PASTA FRA DIAVOLO

BRIO TUSCAN GRILLE > 1601 South Lindbergh Boulevard • Frontenac • 314-432-4410 • brioitalian.com

YIELD: 4 SERVINGS

3 tablespoons olive oil

3 to 4 tablespoons chopped
garlic

1 pound skinless, boneless
chicken breast, grilled and
sliced into bite-size pieces
(shrimp can be substituted)

2 teaspoons red pepper
flakes or more to taste

1½ cups prepared Alfredo
sauce

3 cups prepared marinara
sauce

2 tablespoons lobster base

6 tablespoons (¾ stick)
unsalted butter

1 pound penne, cooked al
dente, drained and kept
hot

Salt

Ground black pepper

½ cup sliced green onions

In a large pot, heat oil over medium heat. Add garlic, chicken and pepper flakes, and sauté 1 minute. Add Alfredo and marinara sauces and simmer for 2 minutes. Add lobster base and whisk until dissolved; stir in butter and hot pasta. Continue to simmer 3 minutes, stirring until butter has melted. Season to taste with salt and pepper; garnish with green onions.

Per serving:

1,103 calories

51.5g fat

42% calories from fat

20g saturated fat

147mg cholesterol

45g protein

115g carbohydrate

24g sugar

5g fiber

2,374mg sodium

173mg calcium

SOUTHWEST CHICKEN PASTA

ROXANE > 12 North Meramec Ave. • Clayton • 314-721-7700 • roxaneonmeramec.com

YIELD: 4 SERVINGS

1 pound penne pasta

¾ pound smoked chicken, sliced about ¼ inch thick

1½ tablespoons olive oil

1 teaspoon minced garlic

1½ cups Creole corn (see note)

15 cherry tomatoes, halved (about 1½ cups)

⅔ cup white wine

1⅓ cups heavy cream

1 to 2 tablespoons Southwest seasoning blend, or to taste, plus more for garnish

Salt

Cook pasta to al dente according to package directions and drain. Set aside.

Cut chicken into 1- to 2-inch pieces; set aside.

In a large pan, warm oil over medium heat; add garlic. Cook and stir about 2 minutes; do not allow to brown. Add corn, tomatoes and chicken. Increase heat to high and cook about 2 minutes.

Add wine. After bubbling has subsided, let wine reduce slightly, 4 to 5 minutes more. Stir in cream, swirling pan to further reduce liquid and mix ingredients. Stir in seasoning and salt to taste. Cook, stirring often, until sauce has thickened to your preference.

Add pasta and toss to coat thoroughly. Divide among serving dishes, and sprinkle with additional Southwest seasoning.

Note: To make Creole corn, cook and drain 1½ cups frozen corn or drain 1 (15-ounce) can whole-kernel corn. Add ¼ cup diced roasted red peppers and about 2 tablespoons melted butter.

Per serving:

928 calories

44g fat

43% calories from fat

23.5g saturated fat

163mg cholesterol

33g protein

100g carbohydrate

8g sugar

5.5g fiber

440mg sodium

93mg calcium

631mg potassium

CHICKEN EMIL

RICH AND CHARLIE'S has a number of locations. • richandcharlies.com

YIELD: 4 LUNCH OR 2 DINNER SERVINGS

¾ cup (1½ sticks) softened butter, divided

2 tablespoons all-purpose flour

2 boneless, skinless chicken breast halves (about 8 ounces each)

½ cup Italian-seasoned dry bread crumbs

1½ cups chicken stock

¾ cup thinly sliced mushrooms (about 3 ounces)

1 cup broccoli florets (see note)

2 tablespoons chopped prosciutto (about 1 slice)

1 clove garlic, chopped

1 pinch red pepper flakes

Juice of ½ lemon (about 2 tablespoons)

½ cup dry white wine

2 cups shredded provel (8 ounces), divided

Preheat oven to 350 degrees. Melt ¼ cup butter; set aside.

In a bowl, combine the remaining ½ cup butter with flour, using the back of a fork or a pastry blender to mix until creamy.

Rinse chicken and pat dry. Cut each piece of chicken in half. Coat chicken with bread crumbs, pressing firmly. Drizzle coated chicken with melted butter; grill or broil for about 5 minutes per side or until fully cooked. Keep chicken warm while you make the sauce.

In a large ovenproof skillet, bring stock to a boil; whisk in butter-flour mixture. Bring to a boil and cook, stirring, until mixture thickens. Reduce to a simmer. Add mushrooms, broccoli, prosciutto, garlic, red pepper flakes, lemon juice and wine. Simmer 5 minutes.

Place cooked chicken pieces in sauce; sprinkle cheese on top of each chicken piece, dividing evenly. Place in oven and bake just until cheese melts, 3 to 4 minutes.

Lift chicken onto plates; use a slotted spoon to ladle vegetables over cheese. Pour sauce over all; serve immediately.

Note: If using fresh broccoli, cut florets and steam or microwave just until crisp-tender. If using frozen broccoli spears or florets, thaw and drain well.

Tester's note: The sauce may be started about 30 minutes ahead. Prepare as directed, but do not add mushrooms and broccoli. Just before serving, add vegetables and simmer until hot, about 7 minutes.

Per lunch serving:

756 calories

56g fat

67% calories from fat

33g saturated fat

220mg cholesterol

44g protein

19g carbohydrate

3g sugar

1g fiber

1,295mg sodium

472mg calcium

454mg potassium

CHICKEN SORRENTINO

TRATTORIA BRANICA > 451 South Kirkwood Road • Kirkwood • 314-909-7575 **/** 10411 Clayton Road • Frontenac • 314-432-8585 • trattoriabranica.com

YIELD: 4 LUNCH OR 2 DINNER SERVINGS

1 small eggplant (preferably Japanese eggplant)

6 tablespoons light-flavored olive oil, divided

1 pound boneless, skinless chicken breast halves

About ⅓ cup all-purpose flour

1 large ripe tomato, chopped

3 to 4 cloves garlic, minced

Salt

Ground black pepper

½ cup white wine

¾ cup chicken broth

¼ cup (½ stick) unsalted butter

3 ounces (about ¾ cup) shredded fontina or mozzarella cheese

Preheat oven to 375 degrees. Peel eggplant and slice lengthwise about ½ inch thick. Place a large nonstick, ovenproof skillet over high heat; when pan is hot, add 2 tablespoons of oil, swirling to coat pan. Add eggplant and sear about 2 minutes on each side; remove from skillet and set aside.

Pound chicken to a uniform thickness of about ½ inch; cut into serving-size pieces. Dredge chicken in flour and shake off excess. Add remaining 4 tablespoons oil to skillet and place over high heat; sauté chicken about 3 minutes, turning to brown lightly on each side.

Add tomato, garlic, salt and pepper to pan; stir in wine, broth and butter. Cook about 6 minutes, until tomato has softened.

Arrange eggplant on chicken, then top with cheese. Transfer to oven; bake about 5 minutes, long enough to heat eggplant and melt cheese. (This dish can also be finished on top of the stove. After adding cheese, cover the pan with a lid, reduce heat to medium and continue cooking just until cheese melts.)

Arrange on serving plates; spoon sauce over all.

Per lunch serving:

595 calories

42g fat

64% calories from fat

15g saturated fat

119mg cholesterol

31g protein

18g carbohydrate

5g sugar

5g fiber

420mg sodium

156mg calcium

620mg potassium

CHICKEN MARSALA

FRATELLI'S RISTORANTE > 2061 Zumbehl Road • St. Charles • 636-949-9005 • fratellisristorante.com

YIELD: 4 SERVINGS

For Marsala sauce:

3 tablespoons olive oil

½ cup diced onion

½ cup chopped green bell pepper

1 tablespoon chopped garlic

8 ounces sliced mushrooms

¼ cup all-purpose flour

½ cup dry Marsala

1½ cups beef stock

⅔ cup tomato sauce

1 tablespoon tomato paste

Salt

Ground black pepper

For chicken:

4 boneless, skinless chicken breast halves

Kosher salt

Freshly ground black pepper

2 eggs, beaten

2 to 3 cups Italian-seasoned dry bread crumbs

3 to 4 tablespoons olive oil, divided

To prepare sauce: Heat oil in a large, heavy sauté pan over medium-high heat. Add onion, green pepper, garlic and mushrooms. Sauté until mushrooms are tender, about 5 minutes. Sprinkle in flour; cook 1 minute. Pour in Marsala, scraping the bottom of the pan with a wooden spoon to release the browned bits. Stir in stock, tomato sauce and tomato paste. Cook until slightly thickened. Add salt and pepper to taste; set aside and keep warm.

To prepare chicken: Rinse chicken and pat dry; place one breast half between sheets of plastic wrap and pound chicken to a uniform ½-inch thickness. Repeat with remaining chicken pieces. Salt and pepper chicken to taste; dip in beaten egg, then lightly coat both sides with bread crumbs.

In a large skillet, heat 1½ tablespoons oil over medium heat. Slowly add chicken in a single layer; cook until golden brown, about 5 minutes. Turn and cook second side until golden, adding oil and cooking in batches as needed.

To serve, place chicken on serving plate. Spoon hot sauce over chicken.

Per serving:

652 calories

29.5g fat

41% calories from fat

4.5g saturated fat

168mg cholesterol

37.5g protein

54g carbohydrate

9g sugar

4g fiber

1,961mg sodium

174mg calcium

862mg potassium

CHICKEN AMARETTO

MARCIANO'S was in West Port Plaza.

YIELD: 1 SERVING

1 (6- to 8-ounce) boneless,
  skinless chicken breast half
  (see note)

1 tablespoon olive oil

¼ cup Italian-seasoned
  bread crumbs

1 tablespoon pine nuts

1 tablespoon butter

½ cup sliced fresh
  mushrooms

⅔ cup beef broth

1 tablespoon tomato sauce

2 tablespoons amaretto

1 tablespoon cornstarch

Prepare a medium fire in the grill. Rinse chicken and pat dry; coat with olive oil, then with bread crumbs. Grill until cooked through.

Toast pine nuts in a dry skillet, stirring frequently; transfer to a small bowl. Melt butter in the skillet. Add mushrooms; sauté for 2 to 3 minutes. Stir together broth, tomato sauce, amaretto and cornstarch; add to mushrooms. Cook, stirring, over medium heat until thickened. Pour over chicken; garnish with pine nuts.

Note: Marciano's served one breast half for a lunch serving, two for dinner.

Per serving:

723 calories

37g fat

46% calories from fat

11g saturated fat

124mg cholesterol

41.5g protein

42.5g carbohydrate

15.5g sugar

2g fiber

1,412mg sodium

94mg calcium

591mg potassium

CHICKEN SPIEDINI

RIZZO'S PASTA > 104 Triad Center West • O'Fallon, Mo. • 636-272-7474

YIELD: 4 SERVINGS

¼ cup lemon juice

3 tablespoons minced fresh garlic

1 teaspoon salt or to taste

½ teaspoon ground black pepper or to taste

¼ cup dried parsley flakes, crumbled

2 pounds chicken, cut into 1½-inch cubes

¾ cup grated Parmesan cheese

About 1 cup Italian-seasoned dry bread crumbs, divided

4 teaspoons butter, melted

8 lemon wedges

In a large bowl, stir together lemon juice, garlic, salt, pepper and parsley flakes. Add chicken; stir to combine. Cover and allow to marinate 1 hour at room temperature.

Meanwhile, if not using the broiler, prepare a fire in the grill.

Toss together Parmesan and ¾ cup bread crumbs. Add chicken; mix well. Thread cubes onto skewers, leaving a little space between the cubes. Roll skewers in additional bread crumbs, just to coat lightly.

Grill or broil, turning once or twice, until chicken is firm and crumbs are toasted, about 25 minutes.

Arrange on serving plates, drizzle with melted butter and garnish with lemon wedges.

Per serving (made with white meat):

439 calories

15g fat

31% calories from fat

6.5g saturated fat

149mg cholesterol

55g protein

21g carbohydrate

2g sugar

1g fiber

1,159mg sodium

262mg calcium

431mg potassium

ENCHILADAS DE CRÈMA

ARCELIA'S > 2001 Park Avenue • St. Louis • 314-231-9200

YIELD: 4 SERVINGS

For sour cream sauce:

4 fresh tomatillos, hulls removed

2 poblano peppers, divided

3 fresh jalapeño peppers, divided

Vegetable oil, for deep-frying

1 red tomato, quartered

2 cups sour cream

2 cloves garlic or to taste, minced

Salt

For enchiladas:

1 to 2 poblano peppers

Vegetable oil, for deep-frying

8 corn tortillas

1½ cups shredded Chihuahua cheese

Chopped fresh cilantro

To prepare sour cream sauce: In a medium pot, combine tomatillos, 1 poblano pepper and 2 jalapeños; cover with water and bring to a boil over medium-high heat. Boil until tender, about 10 minutes. Strain; discard liquid.

Deep-fry remaining poblano and jalapeño at medium heat until skin blisters, about 3 to 4 minutes per side. Remove from oil and plunge into cold water; when cool enough to handle, remove skins. (For milder sauce, remove seeds from peppers; for hotter sauce, leave them in.)

In a blender or food processor, combine boiled vegetables, skinned peppers and red tomato; process until well blended. Stir into sour cream. Add garlic and salt to taste.

To prepare enchiladas: Preheat oven to 350 degrees.

Deep-fry poblanos at medium heat until skin blisters, about 3 to 4 minutes per side. Remove from oil and plunge into cold water; when cool enough to handle, remove skins and seeds; cut into 16 strips and set aside.

Brush each tortilla lightly with hot oil to keep pliable. Place 2 poblano strips on each tortilla; add 2 to 3 tablespoons sauce. Roll up and place enchiladas in a single layer in a baking dish; top with a generous layer of the remaining sauce, then cheese. Bake until warmed through and cheese has melted, 15 minutes. Garnish with cilantro.

Per serving:

933 calories

49g fat

47% calories from fat

24g saturated fat

95mg cholesterol

21g protein

102g carbohydrate

5g sugar

10g fiber

611mg sodium

433mg calcium

665mg potassium

CAYO CHICKEN

WAPANGO > 2020 Chesterfield Mall • Chesterfield • 636-536-1151 • wapango.com

YIELD: 4 SERVINGS

4 boneless, skinless chicken breast halves (6 to 8 ounces each)

2 plum tomatoes

¼ medium white onion, diced

1 tablespoon minced jalapeño

2 tablespoons chopped cilantro

1½ teaspoons chopped garlic

1 tablespoon lime juice

1 teaspoon olive oil

1 teaspoon kosher salt

1½ cups chopped fresh pineapple, drained

About ½ cup jerk seasoning or less to taste

¼ cup (½ stick) butter

Fried onion straws, for optional garnish

Prepare a medium-hot fire in grill (or use a stovetop grill pan). Cook chicken until done. Set aside. (If making ahead, cover and refrigerate.)

Chop tomatoes into ⅜-inch pieces; place in colander and allow to drain for 5 minutes. In a bowl, combine onion, jalapeño, cilantro, garlic, lime juice, olive oil and salt. Add tomatoes and toss to mix well. Measure ½ cup of this mixture into a large bowl. (Refrigerate the remainder for other uses.) Stir pineapple into tomato mixture. Set aside.

Coat all sides of grilled chicken liberally with jerk seasoning; return to grill and cook to form a crust and heat through, 2 to 3 minutes on each side.

In a medium skillet, melt butter; add pineapple mixture and cook over medium heat just until warm. Arrange chicken on serving plates; top with pineapple mixture. If desired, stack fried onion straws on top for garnish.

Note: Wapango serves this on a foundation of pearl pasta in a spicy cream sauce.

Per serving:

324 calories

16g fat

44% calories from fat

8g saturated fat

124mg cholesterol

35g protein

10g carbohydrate

7g sugar

1g fiber

2,126mg sodium

35mg calcium

448mg potassium

WHITE CHICKEN CHILI

BIG BEAR GRILL > 10017 Manchester Road • Warson Woods • 314-821-1000 **/** 16524 Manchester Road • Wildwood • 636-405-1100 • bigbeargrill.com

YIELD: 8 SERVINGS (ABOUT 1 CUP EACH)

9 to 10 ounces boneless, skinless chicken breast

1 tablespoon vegetable oil

2 tablespoons chopped garlic

½ small onion, diced

2½ tablespoons chili powder

1 tablespoon plus 2½ teaspoons ground cumin

1 tablespoon plus 2½ teaspoons dried oregano

2½ tablespoons diced fresh jalapeño peppers

5½ cups chicken stock

3 (15- to 16-ounce) cans Great Northern beans

Shredded Monterey Jack cheese, for garnish

Minced red onion, for garnish

Grill or broil chicken, or cook on a grill pan until done. Cut into bite-size pieces. Set aside.

Heat oil in a large pot over medium heat. Add garlic and diced onion; sauté just until onion is translucent. Do not allow onion to brown. Stir in chili powder, cumin, oregano and jalapeño; cook until seasonings begin to give off a toasted aroma, about 4 minutes. Add stock.

Rinse and drain 1 can beans; add to pot along with 2 cans undrained beans and their liquid. Stir well. Add chicken. Bring to a simmer over low heat; cook 30 minutes.

Garnish each serving with cheese and red onions.

Per serving:
318 calories
6g fat
17% calories from fat
1g saturated fat
23mg cholesterol
23g protein
43g carbohydrate
3g sugar
10g fiber
286mg sodium
135mg calcium
872mg potassium

GRILLED CHICKEN AND MUSHROOM RISOTTO

SOFIA BISTRO was located on Pershing Avenue in St. Louis.

YIELD: 6 SERVINGS (ABOUT 1½ CUPS EACH)

5 cups chicken stock

½ cup (1 stick) butter, divided

1 yellow onion, diced

4 cups sliced cremini mushrooms

2 cups arborio rice

1½ pounds chicken, grilled and diced

1 cup diced fresh tomatoes

1 cup chopped green onion

½ cup grated or shaved pecorino Romano cheese, divided

Salt

Ground black pepper

Chopped fresh parsley, for garnish

Bring chicken stock to a simmer in a saucepan.

In a heavy skillet, melt ¼ cup butter; add onion and sauté until translucent. Add mushrooms; cook 4 minutes. Add rice and cook for 2 to 3 minutes, stirring frequently.

Add 1 cup of the simmering stock, and cook, stirring, until liquid is absorbed. Continue to stir in stock, 1 cup at a time, until rice is just tender, about 20 minutes, stirring frequently.

Gently fold in chicken, tomatoes, green onion, the remaining ¼ cup butter and ¼ cup cheese. Season to taste with salt and pepper. Serve, sprinkling with parsley and the remaining ¼ cup cheese.

Per serving:

499 calories

23g fat

41% calories from fat

13g saturated fat

119mg cholesterol

36g protein

37g carbohydrate

6g sugar

1.5g fiber

521mg sodium

163mg calcium

739mg potassium

TRIPLE MUSTARD AND PECAN CHICKEN SALAD

LA BONNE BOUCHÉE FRENCH BAKERY AND CAFÉ > 12344 Olive Boulevard • Creve Coeur • 314-576-6606 • labonnebouchee.com

YIELD: 8 SERVINGS (ABOUT 6½ CUPS)

2½ pounds skinless, boneless chicken breasts

1½ tablespoons extra-virgin olive oil

¼ cup mustard seeds

¾ cup mayonnaise

1½ tablespoons Pommery mustard (see note)

3 tablespoons Dijon mustard

3 tablespoons fresh lemon juice

¾ teaspoon salt or to taste

3/8 teaspoon freshly ground black pepper

4 ribs celery, diced

¾ cup chopped pecans

Place chicken in a pot; cover with cold water. Bring to a boil over medium-high heat, then reduce heat. Simmer about 10 minutes, until chicken is cooked through. Remove from water and let cool.

Add olive oil to a small skillet. Add mustard seeds; cook over moderate heat, shaking pan until seeds begin to pop, 1 to 2 minutes. Remove skillet from heat and continue to shake until seeds are toasted, fragrant and popping has stopped. Let cool.

In a small bowl, whisk together mayonnaise, Pommery mustard, Dijon mustard, lemon juice, salt and pepper.

Cut chicken into ½-inch cubes. In a large bowl, combine chicken, celery and pecans; add mayonnaise mixture, tossing to coat well. Scrape mustard seeds and oil into bowl and toss again. Taste and adjust seasonings.

Note: Pommery mustard, made in Meaux, France, is a grainy mustard traditionally packed in crocks. It can be found in gourmet and specialty stores and online.

Per serving:

436 calories
32g fat
66% calories from fat
4.5g saturated fat
86mg cholesterol
31g protein
6g carbohydrate
1g sugar
2.5g fiber
596mg sodium
58mg calcium
323mg potassium

117

CHICKEN SALAD

SHRINE RESTAURANT > National Shrine of Our Lady of the Snows • 442 South De Mazenod Drive • Belleville • 618-394-6237 • snows.org

YIELD: 8 CUPS

¼ cup chicken base

3 to 4 cups water

2½ pounds skinless, boneless chicken breasts

2¼ cups mayonnaise

¼ cup plus 2 tablespoons granulated sugar

⅛ teaspoon ground white pepper

½ cup diced celery

½ pound seedless green grapes, cut in half

⅔ cup sliced almonds, toasted

Croissants or lettuce, for serving

In a large pot, stir chicken base into 3 cups water until dissolved. Add chicken and enough water to cover. Place over medium-high heat. Cook until no trace of pink appears when you cut into the thickest part of the chicken. Remove chicken; let cool. (Use broth for soup or sauce or freeze for future use.)

In a large bowl, stir together mayonnaise, sugar and white pepper. Chop chicken into bite-size pieces and add to mayonnaise mixture along with celery, grapes and almonds. Stir gently to combine. Serve on croissants or lettuce.

Per ½-cup serving:

344 calories

28g fat

73% calories from fat

4g saturated fat

50mg cholesterol

15g protein

8g carbohydrate

7g sugar

1g fiber

307mg sodium

20mg calcium

184mg potassium

SNACKS AND
STARTERS

SALADS, SOUPS,
SIDES AND SAUCES

MAIN DISHES

DESSERTS AND
BAKED GOODS

CURRIED CHICKEN SALAD

TEA ROOM IN THE VALLEY > 505 Meramec Station Road • Valley Park • 636-225-4832 • tearoominthevalley.com

YIELD: 7 SERVINGS (EACH ABOUT ¾ CUP)

1 Granny Smith apple, peeled
and coarsely chopped

2 teaspoons lemon juice

4 cups diced cooked chicken

½ cup sliced celery

½ cup slivered almonds

½ teaspoon salt

1 cup mayonnaise

½ teaspoon curry powder

1 tablespoon milk

Place apple in a large bowl. Sprinkle with lemon juice and toss to mix. Gently stir in chicken, celery and almonds. Sprinkle with salt.

In a small bowl, combine mayonnaise and curry powder; stir in milk. Toss with chicken mixture; refrigerate until cold.

Per serving:

416 calories

32g fat

69% calories from fat

5g saturated fat

80mg cholesterol

27g protein

5g carbohydrate

2g sugar

1g fiber

438mg sodium

40mg calcium

302mg potassium

CHICKEN SALAD PIE

MISS AIMEE B'S TEA ROOM > 837 First Capitol Drive • St. Charles • 636-946-4202 • missaimeeb.com

YIELD: 6 SERVINGS

Pastry for a 9-inch deep-dish pie crust

2 eggs

2 cups diced cooked chicken

½ cup shredded Cheddar cheese

¼ cup chopped water chestnuts

½ cup chopped celery

¼ cup finely chopped onion

½ cup canned condensed cream of chicken soup (undiluted)

½ cup sour cream

½ cup mayonnaise

2 tablespoons all-purpose flour

2 tablespoons Cherchies Champagne Mustard (see note)

Preheat oven to 350 degrees. Line pie plate with pastry; prick crust lightly. Line with waxed paper, and fill with pie weights or dried beans. Bake until set but not brown, about 7 to 10 minutes. Remove paper and pie weights or beans.

In a large bowl, beat eggs lightly. Add chicken, cheese, water chestnuts, celery, onion, condensed soup, sour cream, mayonnaise, flour and mustard; mix well. Fill crust with chicken mixture. Bake 45 to 50 minutes or until slightly browned. Serve warm.

Note: The Cherchies mustard is essential to this recipe. It is sold online at cherchies.com and in some local gourmet and grocery stores.

Per serving:

469 calories

33g fat

63% calories from fat

10.5g saturated fat

145mg cholesterol

22g protein

21g carbohydrate

1g sugar

0.5g fiber

515mg sodium

115mg calcium

253mg potassium

PISTACHIO-CRUSTED RUBY TROUT WITH PARSLEY POTATOES AND MISSOURI SWEET CORN BEURRE BLANC

KITCHEN K BAR AND RESTAURANT was on Washington Avenue in St. Louis.

YIELD: 4 SERVINGS

2 pounds new red potatoes, quartered

Salt

2 medium ears corn (see note)

2 tablespoons minced shallots

1 cup white wine

2 tablespoons granulated sugar

¼ cup heavy (whipping) cream

1 cup (2 sticks) plus 3 tablespoons cold unsalted butter, divided

Ground black pepper

4 ruby trout fillets (about 8 ounces each; see note)

½ pound shelled pistachios (about 1 cup), chopped medium-coarse

½ cup chopped flat-leaf parsley

In a large pot, cover potatoes with water; add salt to taste and bring to a boil. Cook until soft, about 20 minutes, stirring occasionally. Remove from heat, drain and cool.

To make beurre blanc, cut kernels from corn cobs. In a medium pot over medium-high heat, sauté corn and shallots until corn starts to brown, 2 to 3 minutes. Add wine, sugar and cream; reduce heat to medium. Simmer until sauce reduces by half, stirring occasionally.

Cut 1 cup cold butter into cubes; gradually whisk into sauce. Add salt and pepper to taste. Remove from heat and keep warm.

Preheat oven to 400 degrees. On a greased baking sheet, place trout fillets skin side down; salt and pepper fillets lightly, and cover skinless side with crushed pistachios. Roast 15 to 20 minutes, until fish flakes easily.

In a large sauté pan over medium-high heat, melt remaining 3 tablespoons butter. Add cooked potatoes, 1 tablespoon salt, 1½ teaspoons pepper and parsley. Sauté potatoes until golden brown, stirring occasionally.

Divide potatoes among serving plates. Arrange trout over potatoes; top with sauce and serve.

Note: You may substitute 1 (15-ounce) can corn, drained, in place of fresh. It will take 5 to 8 minutes to brown. This recipe also works well with rainbow trout or salmon.

Per serving:
1,296 calories
91g fat
63% calories from fat
42g saturated fat
295mg cholesterol
45g protein
69g carbohydrate
15g sugar
11g fiber
1,876mg sodium
153mg calcium
2,382mg potassium

PAN BAGNAT (TUNA SANDWICH)

FRANCO > 1535 South Eighth Street • St. Louis • 314-436-2500 • eatatfranco.com

YIELD: 5 SERVINGS

¼ cup plus 2 tablespoons red wine vinegar

½ ounce fresh basil (about ½ cup loosely packed leaves)

1 ounce flat-leaf parsley (about 1 cup loosely packed leaves)

4 anchovy fillets

1 jalapeño, roasted, peeled and seeded

1 cup extra-virgin olive oil

3 (6-ounce) cans tuna in oil, drained

½ cup diced red onion

½ cup peeled, seeded and diced fresh tomatoes (see note)

½ cup diced roasted red pepper

½ cup chopped Kalamata olives (about 20 olives)

2 hard-cooked eggs, diced

2½ tablespoons capers, drained

1 tablespoon minced garlic

French baguette

Fresh arugula or spinach

Prepare dressing. Combine vinegar, basil, parsley, anchovies, jalapeño and oil in a blender; process until smooth. (Yield: about 1¾ cups.)

Prepare salad. Flake tuna into a large bowl. Add onion, tomatoes, red pepper, olives, eggs, capers and garlic. Mix gently but well.

Add dressing to taste and stir well. Serve on a crusty baguette with fresh arugula or spinach.

Note: To peel tomatoes, bring a pot of water to a boil. Remove from heat, add the tomatoes and let sit for a few minutes, until the peels slip off easily.

Per serving (salad and dressing only):

704 calories
60g fat
77% calories from fat
9g saturated fat
106mg cholesterol
34.5g protein
6.5g carbohydrate
2g sugar
1.5g fiber
940mg sodium
73mg calcium
453mg potassium

SHRIMP PAN ROAST

PEARL'S OYSTER BAR > Ameristar Casino • St. Charles • 636-940-4964 • ameristar.com/stcharles

YIELD: 6 SERVINGS

1 cup diced tomatoes

2 cups tomato purée

3 (8-ounce) bottles clam juice

1 teaspoon minced garlic

1 teaspoon dried oregano

1 teaspoon dried thyme

1 teaspoon dried basil

½ teaspoon Tabasco sauce

1¼ teaspoons kosher salt

1 teaspoon ground black pepper

1 teaspoon paprika

2¼ pounds medium shrimp, peeled and deveined (see note)

2¼ cups 40 percent ("gourmet") whipping cream

3 cups hot white rice mixed with diced bell peppers and onions

In a large pot or Dutch oven, combine tomatoes, tomato purée, clam juice, garlic, oregano, thyme, basil, Tabasco, salt, black pepper and paprika. Bring to a simmer, then cook, uncovered, for 20 minutes or until reduced slightly.

In a large nonstick skillet, cook shrimp over medium heat just until they begin to turn pink.

Add shrimp to pot of sauce; return sauce to a simmer. Stir in cream, then cook about 2 minutes more. Ladle over rice and serve immediately.

Note: You may substitute cooked and drained chunks of andouille sausage, crab claw meat, oysters, cooked chicken or any combination for the shrimp.

Per serving:

575 calories

35g fat

55% calories from fat

21g saturated fat

379mg cholesterol

33g protein

32g carbohydrate

5g sugar

3g fiber

1,310mg sodium

162mg calcium

980mg potassium

BACALAO A LA VIZCAINA

GUIDO'S PIZZERIA AND TAPAS > 5048 Shaw Avenue • St. Louis (the Hill) • 314-771-4900 • guidosstl.com

YIELD: 2 SERVINGS

Salt

2 (8-ounce) cod loins, thawed if frozen

All-purpose flour

3 tablespoons Spanish olive oil

2 slices onion, about ½ inch thick

1 cup canned diced tomatoes

Ground black pepper

Piquillo peppers (see note) or pimientos, drained, for garnish

Preheat oven to 450 degrees.

Lightly salt cod; cut each loin into 2 or 3 pieces. Dust all over with flour. Add olive oil to a skillet and place over medium heat; add cod and cook until lightly browned on each side, about 2 minutes a side. Transfer to a clay baking dish; set aside.

Strain olive oil used to fry cod, wipe skillet clean and return oil to pan. Add onion; cook until translucent, about 5 minutes. Add tomato; cook until most of the liquid has reduced. Add salt and pepper to taste. Pour tomato mixture over cod. Bake, uncovered, for 15 minutes. Before serving, top with 2 or 3 strips of piquillo pepper or pimientos.

Note: Spanish piquillo peppers are similar to a roasted red bell pepper, but are spicier. They are sold in cans and jars in ethnic markets and other specialty shops.

Per serving:

380 calories

22.5g fat

53% calories from fat

3g saturated fat

86mg cholesterol

37g protein

7.5g carbohydrate

4.5g sugar

1.5g fiber

414mg sodium

31mg calcium

437mg potassium

POACHED SALMON

GOURMET TO GO > 9828 Clayton Road • Ladue • 314-993-5442 **/** 7807 Clayton Road • Clayton • 314-727-2442 • gourmettogo.com

YIELD: 4 SERVINGS

SNACKS AND
STARTERS

SALADS, SOUPS,
SIDES AND SAUCES

MAIN DISHES

DESSERTS AND
BAKED GOODS

For salmon:

1 bay leaf

4 to 6 whole peppercorns

Stems from 1 bunch parsley

3 or 4 sprigs fresh thyme

1½ cups white wine

¼ cup coarsely chopped
carrot

½ small onion, cut into
wedges

¼ cup chopped celery

4 (7- to 8-ounce) salmon
fillets

For aspic:

1 cup cold water

3 tablespoons unflavored dry
gelatin

4 thin slices cucumber

4 sprigs dill

To prepare salmon: To make a bouquet garni, cut a double thickness of cheesecloth about 10 inches square. Place bay leaf, peppercorns, parsley stems and thyme in center of cloth; gather corners and tie loosely.

In a deep pan large enough to hold salmon in a single layer, add water to a depth of 2 inches. Add wine, carrot, onion, celery and bouquet garni. Bring to a boil; add salmon and bring to a low simmer. Poach until fish flakes easily, about 10 minutes. (Cook about 10 minutes per inch of thickness, measured at the thickest point.) Lift salmon from pan with a slotted spoon or egg turner. Cover and chill (see note).

To prepare aspic: Place cold water in a small saucepan; sprinkle evenly with gelatin. Let stand 5 minutes. Set pan over medium-low heat; whisk frequently until gelatin has dissolved completely. (Do not allow the mixture to boil.) Remove from heat and let cool until no longer hot, but not yet beginning to set. Spoon over cold salmon to cover entire surface; arrange a cucumber slice and a dill sprig in the aspic over each fillet and chill for a few minutes. When first layer has set, coat with a second layer of aspic.

Note: If desired, salmon may be served immediately; omit the aspic.

Per serving:

353 calories

14g fat

36% calories from fat

2g saturated fat

125mg cholesterol

56g protein

no carbohydrate

no sugar

no fiber

101mg sodium

30mg calcium

1,124mg potassium

CAJUN SHRIMP

LOTAWATA CREEK SOUTHERN GRILL > 311 Salem Place • Fairview Heights • 618-628-7373 • lotawata.com

YIELD: 5 SERVINGS

1 cup (2 sticks) butter, melted

1 cup olive oil

½ cup chili sauce

½ cup Worcestershire sauce

3 tablespoons chopped garlic

¼ cup Creole seasoning

¼ cup lemon juice

¼ cup chopped parsley

2¼ teaspoons paprika

2¼ teaspoons ground red (cayenne) pepper

2¼ teaspoons dried oregano

1¼ teaspoons Louisiana hot sauce

2½ pounds in-shell shrimp (23- to 30-count)

2½ lemons, cut into wedges, for garnish

Bread, for dipping

Preheat the oven to 350 degrees. Combine melted butter, oil, chili sauce, Worcestershire sauce, garlic, Creole seasoning, lemon juice, parsley, paprika, cayenne, oregano and hot sauce in a large bowl; mix well. Add shrimp and toss to coat. Place in a shallow pan and bake about 20 minutes or until shrimp are opaque.

Transfer to a serving bowl and garnish with lemon wedges. Serve with sauce and plenty of bread to sop up the sauce.

Per serving (if all the sauce is consumed):

813 calories

81g fat

90% calories from fat

29g saturated fat

160mg cholesterol

10g protein

11g carbohydrate

4g sugar

1g fiber

1,815mg sodium

94mg calcium

548mg potassium

CAJUN SEAFOOD GUMBO

KIRKWOOD ICE AND FUEL > 215 North Kirkwood Road • Kirkwood • 314-822-0494

YIELD: 8 SERVINGS (ABOUT 12 CUPS)

10 cups water

1 (7-ounce) box New Orleans-style black beans and rice (see note)

½ cup diced green bell pepper

½ cup diced red bell pepper

2 small potatoes, diced

3 ribs celery, diced

1 carrot, diced

1 small onion, diced

1 tablespoon Cajun seasoning

1 tablespoon Lawry's seasoned salt

3 dashes Tabasco sauce or to taste

6 ounces shredded cooked chicken

½ pound diced spicy sausage, such as kielbasa or andouille

8 to 10 ounces cooked small (cocktail) shrimp

8 to 10 ounces crabmeat or imitation (surimi) crab

In a large soup pot or Dutch oven, combine water and beans/rice mix. Bring to a boil, reduce heat, cover and simmer 25 minutes, stirring occasionally.

Stir in bell peppers, potatoes, celery, carrot and onion. Cover and simmer 25 minutes more. Stir in Cajun seasoning, seasoned salt and Tabasco, then add chicken, sausage, shrimp and crab. Increase heat and bring to a boil, then reduce heat, cover and simmer 25 minutes more.

Note: Zatarain's Black Beans and Rice mix has seasonings similar to those used at Kirkwood Ice and Fuel.

Per serving:

283 calories

7g fat

22% calories from fat

2.5g saturated fat

79mg cholesterol

26g protein

29g carbohydrate

3g sugar

4g fiber

1,646mg sodium

99mg calcium

473mg potassium

GREEN CURRY MUSSELS

WEST END GRILL AND PUB > 354 North Boyle Avenue • St. Louis • 314-531-4607 • westendgandp.com

YIELD: 2 SERVINGS

3 tablespoons olive oil

½ cup minced red onion

2 tablespoons minced garlic

2 tablespoons minced fresh ginger

1 teaspoon minced fresh jalapeño

1 tablespoon green curry paste

1 cup white wine

1 (14-ounce) can unsweetened coconut milk

1 teaspoon chile paste

1 tablespoon soy sauce

1 tablespoon fresh lime juice

1 cup minced cilantro

1 pound fresh Prince Edward Island mussels, cleaned and debearded (see note)

Bread or crostini, for dipping

In a large pot, heat oil over medium heat; add onion, garlic, ginger and jalapeño. Sauté until onion is translucent, 3 to 4 minutes. Blend curry paste into vegetables; cook about 3 minutes, stirring constantly to "toast" the curry, being careful not to let it burn.

Stir in wine, coconut milk, chile paste, soy sauce, lime juice and cilantro; bring to a boil. Add mussels and cover pot; steam until mussels open, about 3 to 5 minutes. Discard any unopened mussels.

Serve on a large, deep platter with bread or crostini to dip into any leftover broth.

Note: To clean and debeard fresh mussels, scrub them with a stiff brush under cold running water just before cooking. Remove any moss-like bits. Discard any mussels that do not close tightly when tapped on the counter.

Per serving:

976 calories

72g fat

66% calories from fat

41g saturated fat

64mg cholesterol

32g protein

29g carbohydrate

3.5g sugar

3g fiber

1,300mg sodium

122mg calcium

1,360mg potassium

MONGOLIAN BEEF

KING DOH > 10045 Manchester Road • Warson Woods • 314-821-6988 • kingdoh.com

YIELD: 2 SERVINGS

¾ pound flank steak

2 tablespoons lightly beaten egg

2 teaspoons cornstarch

2 to 3 tablespoons plus 2 teaspoons vegetable oil, divided

1 to 2 bunches green onions, cut into 2-inch pieces

2 teaspoons granulated sugar

2 tablespoons soy sauce

Rice noodles, fried and drained (see note)

Cut flank steak lengthwise into three pieces, then cut across the grain into ¼-inch-thick slices. Place in a medium bowl. Stir egg into beef; add cornstarch and 2 teaspoons oil. Mix well. Let stand 15 to 20 minutes.

Place a large skillet over high heat; when pan is hot, add 2 tablespoons oil and beef mixture. Stir-fry until beef has lost all of its pink color; remove with a slotted spoon. Keep meat warm.

Add green onions (and up to 1 tablespoon oil if needed) to skillet; stir-fry until onions soften and become fragrant, about 4 minutes. Add sugar and soy sauce, then return beef to skillet. Stir-fry until flavors are evenly blended, about 3 minutes.

To serve, place a bed of fried rice noodles on a platter; top with Mongolian Beef.

Note: Noodles made of rice flour puff up dramatically when added to a small amount of hot oil; after cooking, drain well. "Cellophane" noodles or "bean threads" (made of mung beans) may be substituted. Stir-fried meat dishes may also be served over shredded cabbage or alongside steamed rice.

Per serving (without noodles):

466 calories

30g fat

58% calories from fat

8g saturated fat

124mg cholesterol

40g protein

9g carbohydrate

7g sugar

no fiber

1,430mg sodium

57mg calcium

595mg potassium

STEAK DIANE

AL'S RESTAURANT > 1200 North First Street • St. Louis • 314-421-6399 • alsrestaurant.net

YIELD: 2 SERVINGS

2 center cut-beef filets
  (about 8 ounces each)

Salt

Freshly ground black pepper

½ cup extra-virgin olive oil

½ cup diced onion

½ cup diced fresh
  mushrooms

1 tablespoon minced garlic

1 tablespoon cornstarch

1¼ cups rich beef stock
  (see note)

1 tablespoon Worcestershire
  sauce

½ cup dry red wine

2 tablespoons minced fresh
  parsley

Season filets to taste with salt and pepper. Heat a large sauté pan or heavy skillet over medium-high heat; add olive oil. Add steaks and cook about 2 minutes on each side. Transfer partially cooked steaks to a plate.

Drain off all but about 2 tablespoons of the oil; add onion to the pan and sauté until translucent, about 3 minutes. Add mushrooms and garlic, stirring well.

Mix cornstarch into beef stock; add to pan. Stir in Worcestershire sauce. Return steaks to sauce and cook for 3 minutes. Add wine; cook for 3 minutes more. Turn steaks and cook 5 to 6 minutes, until medium-rare.

Arrange steaks on serving plates; drizzle sauce over and garnish with parsley.

Note: If you don't have rich beef stock, use canned broth with about ½ teaspoon beef base dissolved in it.

Per serving:
672 calories
42.5g fat
57% calories from fat
13g saturated fat
147mg cholesterol
47g protein
14.5g carbohydrate
4.5g sugar
1.5g fiber
224mg sodium
76mg calcium
910mg potassium

BRAISED SHORT RIBS

LA BONNE BOUCHÉE > 12344 Olive Boulevard • Creve Coeur • 314-576-6606 • labonnebouchee.com

YIELD: 4 TO 6 SERVINGS

2 tablespoons kosher or sea salt

2 teaspoons freshly cracked black pepper

5 pounds short ribs

1 to 2 tablespoons vegetable oil

1 cup diced onion

2 small carrots, sliced diagonally

1 large rib celery, sliced diagonally

¾ cup bread or all-purpose flour

2 cups red wine

2 quarts beef broth

1 bay leaf

6 sprigs fresh thyme

¼ cup cornstarch mixed with ⅓ cup water or 5 tablespoons flour stirred into 4 tablespoons melted butter

Preheat oven to 275 degrees. Stir together salt and pepper, then season short ribs all over.

Place a large, heavy Dutch oven over high heat; add oil. When oil begins to smoke, add short ribs and sear to brown on all sides; remove ribs from pan and set aside.

Turn heat to medium. Add onion, carrots and celery to the pan; cook until vegetables start to caramelize, about 10 minutes.

Whisk together flour and wine; add to vegetables and stir to coat. Add beef broth, bay leaf and thyme. Stir until liquid is smooth.

Return short ribs to pan; cover pan. Transfer to oven and bake about 2 hours or until meat is very tender. When tender, remove meat from pan and hold in a warm place.

Strain braising liquid into a saucepot. Add cornstarch slurry or flour-butter roux. Cook over medium heat until thickened, stirring often. Adjust seasoning with salt and pepper. Cut ribs into serving-size portions; serve with sauce and vegetables. (Ribs may be held at serving temperature in completed sauce.)

Per serving (based on 6):

1,007 calories

79g fat

71% calories from fat

32g saturated fat

165mg cholesterol

44g protein

23g carbohydrate

2.5g sugar

1.5g fiber

3,080mg sodium

64mg calcium

760mg potassium

ROPA VIEJA (CUBAN BEEF BRISKET)

KITCHEN K BAR AND RESTAURANT was on Washington Avenue in St. Louis.

YIELD: 8 TO 12 SERVINGS

1 tablespoon chopped
cilantro

1½ teaspoons chopped garlic

2 tablespoons chopped green
onions

1 jalapeño, chopped

1 tablespoon vegetable oil

2 to 3 pounds beef brisket,
trimmed of excess fat

1 green bell pepper, seeded
and diced

1 red bell pepper, seeded and
diced

1 red onion, diced

1 poblano pepper, diced

4 green olives

⅓ cup capers, drained

1 cup tomato paste (about
1½ 6-ounce cans)

16 ounces (2 cups) beer

1 cup red wine

1 tablespoon kosher salt

1 teaspoon ground black
pepper

In a food processor fitted with the steel blade, combine cilantro, garlic, green onions, jalapeño and oil; process until puréed.

Cut brisket into 2-inch chunks. In a large heavy pot, combine puréed mixture and beef. Stir in bell peppers, onion, poblano pepper, olives, capers, tomato paste, beer, wine, salt and black pepper. Add water to cover. Bring to a simmer, cover and cook over medium-low heat 2 to 3 hours, until meat is tender and shreds easily.

Per serving (based on 8, made with 2 pounds of brisket):

544 calories

38g fat

63% calories from fat

14g saturated fat

105mg cholesterol

29g protein

12g carbohydrate

6g sugar

2.5g fiber

1,280mg sodium

35mg calcium

740mg potassium

147

TRAILHEAD CHILI WITH SMOKED BRISKET

TRAILHEAD BREWING CO. > 921 South Riverside Drive • St. Charles • 636-946-2739 • trailheadbrewing.com

YIELD: ABOUT 8 (10-OUNCE) SERVINGS

SNACKS AND
STARTERS

SALADS, SOUPS,
SIDES AND SAUCES

MAIN DISHES

DESSERTS AND
BAKED GOODS

1¼ pounds flat-cut beef brisket (see note)

Purchased or homemade rub for pork ribs

¾ cup chopped onion

½ pound tomatoes, chopped

1 (4.5-ounce) can diced green chiles

1¾ cups bottled chili sauce

1¾ cups cooked pinto beans or 1 (15-ounce) can, drained

1½ teaspoons to 1 tablespoon ground red (cayenne) pepper

2¼ teaspoons ground cumin

¾ teaspoon garlic powder

1 teaspoon dried oregano

1½ teaspoons salt

Grated Cheddar-Monterey Jack cheese blend

Coat both sides of meat generously with rib rub. Smoke brisket until internal temperature reaches 160 degrees. Let cool; reserve any juices.

When meat is cool, slice across the grain into ¼-inch slices; cut into ¼-inch cubes. (Brisket may be made in advance to this point; refrigerate up to a day in a tightly covered container.)

In a heavy pot with a lid, combine brisket and onions; cook over medium heat until onions have caramelized, stirring occasionally.

Measure pan juices; add water to equal 2 cups. Add liquid to meat mixture and bring to a boil. Add tomatoes, green chiles, chili sauce, beans, cayenne to taste, cumin, garlic powder, oregano and salt; reduce heat to a simmer. Cover; cook, stirring occasionally, at least 30 minutes. If chili is too thin, remove lid and simmer until liquid reduces. Ladle into bowls; top with cheese.

Notes: Most flat-cut briskets are larger than the amount needed for this recipe. You can smoke the entire piece and double the recipe or make the recipe as it is written and freeze the extra meat. (For best quality, do not dice the meat before freezing.)

If you do not have access to a smoker, preheat oven to 350 degrees. Rub brisket with olive oil. Place a large ovenproof pan with a lid on the stove over medium-high heat. Add brisket; brown on both sides. Sprinkle liberally with liquid smoke on both sides, then sprinkle with rib rub. Cover and bake to an internal temperature of 160 degrees, about 90 minutes. Remove meat from pan and let cool; reserve pan juices.

Per serving (without cheese):

215 calories

3g fat

13% calories from fat

1g saturated fat

30mg cholesterol

19g protein

28g carbohydrate

14g sugar

5g fiber

1,358mg sodium

43mg calcium

497mg potassium

SAUERBRATEN

BEVO MILL, 4749 Gravois Avenue, is under new management.

YIELD: 8 SERVINGS

4 pounds beef eye of round or sirloin roast, trimmed of excess fat

2 medium onions, sliced

1 medium orange, unpeeled and sliced, or 2 cups orange juice

1 teaspoon whole cloves

1 clove garlic

1 bay leaf

1 tablespoon ground ginger

1 teaspoon whole black peppercorns

1/2 teaspoon ground black pepper

1 tablespoon salt

2 cups vinegar

1 cup red wine

1 2/3 cups water, divided

1/3 cup cornstarch

Slice meat about 1 inch thick. Place in a large self-sealing plastic bag.

In a large bowl, combine onions, orange slices or juice, cloves, garlic, bay leaf, ginger, peppercorns, ground pepper, salt, vinegar, wine and 1 cup water. Pour into bag containing meat. Seal bag; place in a clean bowl or pan. Refrigerate for 36 hours, turning bag two or three times.

Remove meat. Strain marinade. In a large skillet, brown meat over medium-high heat. Add enough of the marinade to the skillet to cover the meat. Bring to a simmer, cover and cook over low heat until tender, about 1 to 2 hours.

Remove meat; keep warm. Strain pan juices and return to skillet. Dissolve cornstarch in 2/3 cup cool water. Whisk cornstarch mixture into juices in skillet; cook until thickened slightly. Serve with meat. (Makes about 6 cups sauce.)

Per serving:
411 calories
16.5g fat
36% calories from fat
6g saturated fat
106mg cholesterol
49g protein
14g carbohydrate
6g sugar
1g fiber
510mg sodium
32mg calcium
469mg potassium

151

BEEF TENDERLOIN MEDALLIONS WITH PORT REDUCTION AND GORGONZOLA

THE AMERICAN BOUNTY > 430 West Front Street • Washington, Mo. • 636-390-2150

YIELD: 4 SERVINGS

2 cups ruby port wine

1 cup heavy (whipping) cream

¼ cup (½ stick) unsalted butter

8 (3-ounce) beef tenderloin medallions (do not season)

4 ounces crumbled gorgonzola cheese, divided

In a nonreactive pan, bring the port wine to a simmer over medium-high heat; cook until reduced to ¾ cup. (Be careful if using a gas stove; the evaporating alcohol may ignite.)

Add cream; cook until reduced by half. (You should have ⅞ cup.) Remove from heat and add butter. Constantly swirl the pan while butter melts into the sauce, whisking lightly to incorporate.

Hold the sauce, covered, in a warm place; do not try to reheat.

Grill beef medallions to desired doneness, preferably no more than medium. Arrange two medallions on each plate and surround with about ¼ cup sauce. Top each serving with 1 ounce of the gorgonzola and serve.

Per serving:

565 calories

38g fat

61% calories from fat

21.5g saturated fat

183mg cholesterol

42g protein

6g carbohydrate

2g sugar

1g fiber

467mg sodium

162mg calcium

624mg potassium

BEEF SOTO

RIZZO'S PASTA > 104 Triad Center West • O'Fallon, Mo. • 636-272-7474

YIELD: 2 SERVINGS

6 beef medallions (about
   2 ounces each)

About ¾ cup seasoned dry
   bread crumbs

¾ cup water

2 tablespoons lemon juice

¼ cup Chablis wine

2 teaspoons butter

2 teaspoons all-purpose flour

Salt

Ground black pepper

1½ teaspoons minced garlic

1 teaspoon minced parsley,
   plus extra for garnish

½ cup sliced fresh
   mushrooms

4 ounces provel cheese
   (about 1 cup string provel)

Preheat a grill. Coat beef medallions with bread crumbs. Grill quickly, no more than 1½ minutes on each side. Remove and keep warm.

In a pot, combine water, lemon juice and wine; bring to a boil. Meanwhile, melt butter in a small pan; stir in flour until well combined.

Reduce heat slightly under wine mixture. Whisk in flour mixture. Add salt to taste, a pinch of pepper, garlic, 1 teaspoon parsley and mushrooms. Cook until sauce is thickened and mushrooms are tender, about 8 minutes. Taste and correct seasonings.

Arrange beef on serving plates; top with cheese. Pour hot sauce over cheese. Garnish with minced parsley. Serve immediately.

Per serving:

687 calories

32g fat

42% calories from fat

16.5g saturated fat

147mg cholesterol

57g protein

37.5g carbohydrate

4g sugar

2.5g fiber

1,396mg sodium

534mg calcium

867mg potassium

SNACKS AND
STARTERS

SALADS, SOUPS,
SIDES AND SAUCES

MAIN DISHES

DESSERTS AND
BAKED GOODS

KARNI YARIK (EGGPLANT STUFFED WITH BEEF AND SPICES)

AYA SOFIA > 6671 Chippewa Street • St. Louis • 314-645-9919 • ayasofiacuisine.com

YIELD: 4 SERVINGS

4 Chinese eggplants

Salt

2 tablespoons vegetable oil

2 tablespoons olive oil

4 or 5 cloves garlic

1 medium white onion, chopped

1 tablespoon tomato paste

1 pound ground beef

1 tablespoon freshly ground black pepper

1 teaspoon paprika

3 sprigs parsley, chopped

6 green onions, chopped

2 medium tomatoes (1 chopped and 1 sliced)

1½ cups thick tomato-based pasta sauce, optional

Wash eggplants, then remove strips of peel with a vegetable peeler; eggplants should appear "striped." Halve lengthwise. Scoop out seeds to make a trench for the filling. Soak eggplants in salted water for 30 minutes; dry thoroughly.

Cook eggplants in vegetable oil in a large skillet over high heat until softened, about 5 minutes. Drain on paper towels and let cool.

Preheat oven to 350 degrees.

Heat olive oil in a skillet over medium heat; add garlic and cook until it begins to brown. Add white onion; cook until soft and golden brown. Stir in tomato paste; add ground beef and cook until well done. Stir in 1 tablespoon salt, pepper, paprika, parsley, green onions and chopped tomato; cook for 2 minutes.

Place eggplants side by side in baking pan; divide meat mixture evenly and mound onto eggplants. Place a slice of tomato on top of each stuffed eggplant half. Put a little water in the bottom of the pan to prevent burning. Cover and bake for 15 minutes. Uncover; bake 10 minutes longer, to crisp surface slightly.

If desired, heat the pasta sauce and ladle on before serving.

Per serving:

487 calories

25.5g fat

47% calories from fat

6g saturated fat

67g cholesterol

28g protein

36.5g carbohydrate

20g sugar

13g fiber

1,878mg sodium

623mg potassium

MEATLOAF

SOULARD'S > 1731 South Seventh Street • St. Louis • 314-241-7956 • soulards.com

YIELD: 6 TO 8 SERVINGS

2 pounds ground chuck

½ pound pork sausage

2 eggs

⅔ cup rolled oats

1 tablespoon steak sauce

2 teaspoons ground green peppercorns

1 teaspoon onion powder

1 teaspoon chopped parsley

1 tablespoon seasoned salt

1 teaspoon ground black pepper

1 cup ketchup, divided

6 to 8 slices bacon

Brown gravy, for serving

Preheat oven to 350 degrees.

In a large bowl, combine ground chuck, sausage, eggs, oats, steak sauce, green peppercorns, onion powder, parsley, seasoned salt, pepper and ½ cup ketchup. Mix gently but well. Shape mixture into a loaf about 4½ inches wide, 2½ inches thick and 11 inches long. Put in a shallow baking dish; top loaf with remaining ½ cup ketchup. Arrange bacon slices on top. Bake 35 minutes or until cooked through. Allow to rest for 10 minutes before slicing. Serve with brown gravy.

Per serving (based on 8 servings, without gravy):

358 calories

21g fat

51% calories from fat

7g saturated fat

137mg cholesterol

28g protein

14g carbohydrate

8g sugar

1g fiber

1,273mg sodium

43mg calcium

484mg potassium

KIRBY'S GRANDMA'S MEATLOAF WITH WILD MUSHROOM DEMIGLACE

ELEVEN ELEVEN > 1111 Mississippi Avenue • St. Louis • 314-241-9999 • 1111-m.com

YIELD: 8 SERVINGS

For meatloaf:

1 pound ground beef

1 pound ground veal

3 tablespoons Worcestershire sauce

1 cup ketchup

1 (12-ounce) can diced tomatoes (see note)

3 cups rolled oats

5 eggs, lightly beaten

Salt

Ground black pepper

1 pound bacon

For wild mushroom demiglace:

¼ cup olive oil

1 pound exotic mushrooms, sliced (a mixture of your favorites)

½ pound shallots, sliced

2 cups burgundy wine

1 cup veal demiglace (see note)

To prepare meatloaf: Preheat oven to 300 degrees.

In a large bowl, combine beef, veal, Worcestershire, ketchup, tomatoes and their juice, oats, eggs and salt and pepper to taste. Mix gently but well.

Cut a piece of parchment paper to fit a large shallow pan with sides. Arrange about half the bacon slices down the center of the parchment, long sides just touching. Spoon meat mixture onto the center of the bacon base. Form meat into a loaf about 14 inches long and 5 inches wide; pull ends of bacon slices up to wrap sides of loaf. Place remaining bacon over loaf and tuck ends under. Bake 90 minutes or until juices run clear.

To prepare demiglace: Heat oil in a saucepan. Add mushrooms and shallots; sauté until tender, about 7 minutes. Add wine and cook until only about ¼ cup liquid remains in the pan. Stir in veal demiglace; cook until hot.

Slice meatloaf; serve with demiglace.

Note: If using a 14- to 15-ounce can of tomatoes, discard about ⅓ cup juice. If using purchased veal demiglace concentrate, dilute 2 ½ tablespoons in 1 cup hot water.

Per serving:

461 calories

20g fat

39% calories from fat

5g saturated fat

201mg cholesterol

30.5g protein

38.5g carbohydrate

11g sugar

4g fiber

656mg sodium

57mg calcium

729mg potassium

VEAL PARMIGIANO RIGAZZI'S

RIGAZZI'S > 4945 Daggett Avenue • St. Louis • 314-772-4900 • rigazzis.com

YIELD: 4 SERVINGS

½ pound ground beef

1 (33-ounce) jar pasta sauce

⅓ cup milk

1 egg

4 (4-ounce) veal cutlets
  (see note)

½ cup all-purpose flour

1 cup Italian-seasoned dry
  bread crumbs

6 tablespoons olive oil

8 slices provel cheese

¼ cup Parmesan cheese

In a medium saucepan, cook ground beef until browned, stirring to break it up; drain. Add pasta sauce and simmer until warm.

Preheat oven to 325 degrees. In bowl, blend together milk and egg. Dust veal cutlets with flour, then dip into egg mixture. Cover with bread crumbs, patting to hold firmly.

In a sauté pan over medium heat, warm oil for 2 minutes. Add breaded veal. Cook 3 minutes on each side or until outside is crispy.

Coat the bottom of a small jellyroll pan with about ¾ cup of the meat sauce. Arrange sautéed cutlets over sauce. Top each cutlet with 2 slices of provel. Cover with remaining meat sauce; sprinkle with Parmesan. Bake until cheese is melted, about 10 minutes. Serve immediately.

Note: You can use frozen 4-ounce hamburger patties (do not thaw) in place of the veal.

Per serving:

1,022 calories

58g fat

51% calories from fat

19g saturated fat

214mg cholesterol

59g protein

66g carbohydrate

24g sugar

7.5g fiber

2,358mg sodium

650mg calcium

1,223mg potassium

BRAISED LAMB

CAFÉ NATASHA'S KABOB INTERNATIONAL > 3200 South Grand Boulevard • St. Louis • 314-771-3411 • kabobinternational.com

YIELD: 2 SERVINGS (RECIPE CAN BE DOUBLED)

SNACKS AND
STARTERS

SALADS, SOUPS,
SIDES AND SAUCES

MAIN DISHES

DESSERTS AND
BAKED GOODS

1 lamb shoulder or shank

1 large onion, quartered

2 to 4 bay leaves

2 to 4 cloves garlic, smashed

Ground black pepper

Seasoned salt

½ teaspoon ground
cinnamon

¼ teaspoon ground turmeric

¼ teaspoon ground cumin

½ teaspoon hot or mild curry
paste (see note)

2 tablespoons tomato paste,
optional

½ cup raisins or other
dried fruit (such as figs or
apricots), optional

Rinse lamb; pat dry. Place a heavy soup pot, Dutch oven or large saucepan over medium heat. Add 1 cup water, onion, bay leaves and garlic. Sprinkle the meat with pepper and seasoned salt to taste. Rub meat with cinnamon, turmeric, cumin and curry paste. Add meat to pot. Cover and cook over medium heat about 30 minutes, until mixture is steaming and meat begins to brown lightly.

Add enough cold water to cover the meat; bring to a boil. Reduce heat to a simmer. If desired, add tomato paste and/or dried fruit. Cook 1 to 1½ hours, until meat is very tender and loosened from bones.

When the meat has finished cooking, remove meat from broth. Discard bay leaves. Refrigerate meat and broth separately. When broth is cold, skim and discard any fat.

Reheat broth. If necessary, add garlic, seasoned salt, pepper, cinnamon, cumin and/or curry paste to taste. Return meat to broth; place over medium heat to rewarm or to hold until serving. (Meat may be served as whole lamb shanks or removed from the bone and used as an ingredient in stew or pilaf.)

Variation: After steaming and slightly browning the meat (step 1), transfer the meat and pan juices to a slow cooker and cover meat with water. If desired, add tomato paste and dried fruit. Cook on low until tender, about 8 hours.

Note: Jars of hot and mild curry paste are sold in Asian markets and many supermarkets. We tested this recipe with Taste of Thai brand curry paste.

Per serving:

274 calories

13.5g fat

44% calories from fat

5.5g saturated fat

100mg cholesterol

29g protein

9g carbohydrate

3.5g sugar

2g fiber

86mg sodium

58mg calcium

368mg potassium

PUMPKIN GELATO

CHARLIE GITTO'S ON THE HILL > 5226 Shaw Avenue • St. Louis • 314-772-8898 • charliegittos.com

YIELD: ABOUT 1 QUART

2 cups whole milk

1 cup heavy (whipping) cream

4 egg yolks

½ cup granulated sugar

¼ cup canned pumpkin pie filling (preferred) or canned pumpkin

1 teaspoon ground cinnamon

1 teaspoon ground nutmeg

1 teaspoon ground allspice

Chocolate sauce, optional (see note)

In a heavy medium saucepan, bring milk and cream to a simmer over medium heat. Remove from heat.

In a mixing bowl, stir together yolks and sugar; beat until foamy. Gradually pour the warm milk into yolk mixture, whisking constantly.

Return the mixture to the pan and cook over medium heat, stirring with a wooden spoon until the mixture thickens and coats the back of the spoon. Pour through a sieve or fine strainer into a bowl. Cover and chill completely.

Stir in pumpkin and spices; mix until well-incorporated. Pour into an ice cream maker and freeze according to manufacturer's directions. Transfer to a container, cover and freeze until firm. Serve with chocolate sauce.

Note: To make chocolate sauce, bring 1½ cups heavy (whipping) cream just to a boil in a saucepan over medium heat. Add 6 to 14 ounces semi-sweet chocolate chips, depending on desired thickness. Stir until chocolate melts completely. Pour into a bowl and cool.

YIELD: 8 SERVINGS.

Per serving, made with 6 ounces chocolate: 270 calories; 23g fat; 14g saturated fat; 60mg cholesterol; 2g protein; 15g carbohydrate; 12g sugar; 1g fiber; 20mg sodium; 40mg calcium.

Per ½-cup serving (without sauce):

230 calories

15g fat

59% calories from fat

9g saturated fat

150mg cholesterol

4g protein

19g carbohydrate

16g sugar

1g fiber

60mg sodium

100mg calcium

FRUIT BARS

PARTY PASTRY SHOP > 15447 Clayton Road • Ballwin • 636-227-7188

YIELD: 4 TO 5 DOZEN COOKIES

1⅓ cups packed brown sugar

⅔ cup shortening or butter
(not margarine)

1¾ teaspoons baking soda

1 teaspoon salt

1 teaspoon ground cinnamon

½ cup honey

¼ cup molasses

1 egg

3¼ cups (1 pound)
all-purpose flour

1 pound moist raisins
(about 3 cups)

Preheat the oven to 350 degrees. In a large bowl of an electric mixer, combine sugar, shortening or butter, baking soda, salt, cinnamon, honey and molasses; beat until completely blended, about 4 minutes. Add egg, then beat for about 3 minutes more. Gradually beat in flour, mixing until incorporated. Beat in raisins.

Line a baking sheet that is at least 13 inches long with parchment paper. Divide dough into 7 equal portions (about 7½ ounces each). Shape 1 portion into a 12-inch "log" on parchment. (The shape is not critical, as the dough spreads during baking, but try for a uniform thickness.) Place another log of dough parallel to the first, about 3 inches apart. Repeat with remaining dough.

Bake 12 to 14 minutes; logs will be soft. Cool 5 minutes on pan, then cut each log into 2-inch pieces. Slide the parchment off the pan onto cooling racks. Cool completely.

Tester's note: To prevent excess browning on the bottom, bake in the upper third of the oven, or use two baking sheets (one on top of the other) or use insulated baking sheets.

Per cookie (based on 60):
102 calories
2.5g fat
22% calories from fat
0.5g saturated fat
4mg cholesterol
1g protein
19g carbohydrate
12g sugar
0.5g fiber
80mg sodium
13mg calcium
95mg potassium

SNACKS AND STARTERS

SALADS, SOUPS SIDES AND SAUCES

MAIN DISHES

DESSERTS AND BAKED GOODS

GOOEY BUTTER COOKIES

THE BLUE OWL RESTAURANT AND BAKERY > Second and Mill streets • Kimmswick • 636-464-3128 • theblueowl.com

YIELD: ABOUT 4 DOZEN COOKIES

¼ cup (½ stick) butter,
  softened (do not use
  margarine)

¼ teaspoon vanilla

1 egg

4 ounces cream cheese,
  softened

1 (about-18-ounce) box
  yellow cake mix

1 cup powdered sugar

In large bowl of electric mixer, beat together butter, vanilla, egg and cream cheese until light and fluffy. Add cake mix; beat until well blended. Cover dough and chill 30 minutes.

Preheat oven to 350 degrees. Shape dough into 1-inch balls; roll in powdered sugar. Place about 1½ inches apart on a lightly greased cookie sheet (see note). Bake 12 minutes; do not let brown.

Let cookies cool, then sift additional powdered sugar over the tops.

Tester's note: It isn't necessary to shake off excess powdered sugar after rolling. Baking on a greased sheet results in just enough spreading to make the cookies a perfect two-bite size. If you bake on parchment paper, the cookies spread a bit less and are more ball-shaped. These should not brown; baking 12 minutes allows the cookies to stay soft.

I also tested this with chocolate cake mix with good results. Recipe may be doubled.

Per cookie:

75 calories

3g fat

36% calories from fat

1.5g saturated fat

10mg cholesterol

1g protein

11g carbohydrate

7g sugar

no fiber

80mg sodium

17mg calcium

14mg potassium

GUINNESS BROWNIES

LLYWELYN'S PUB > 4747 McPherson Avenue • St. Louis • 314-361-3003 • and two other locations • llywelynspub.com

YIELD: 16 SERVINGS

4 ounces unsweetened
  chocolate, cut into chunks

¾ cup (1½ sticks) butter

2 cups granulated sugar

3 eggs

1 teaspoon vanilla

1 cup Guinness stout

¾ cup all-purpose flour

Llywelyn's Guinness Fudge
  Sauce (see recipe)

Ice cream or whipped cream

Preheat oven to 350 degrees. Grease a 9-by-13-inch baking pan.

Gradually melt chocolate and butter together in the top of a double-boiler; stir to blend. Remove from heat; stir in sugar, eggs, vanilla and Guinness. Stir in flour. Batter will be thin.

Pour into baking pan; bake until almost set, about 35 minutes. Do not overbake.

Let cool, then slice into 16 bars. Serve with Guinness Fudge Sauce and ice cream or whipped cream.

Per brownie:

257 calories

13g fat

46% calories from fat

8g saturated fat

62mg cholesterol

3g protein

32g carbohydrate

26g sugar

1g fiber

17mg sodium

16mg calcium

81mg potassium

LLYWELYN'S GUINNESS FUDGE SAUCE   YIELD: ABOUT 2¼ CUPS

1 (12-ounce) jar hot
  fudge sauce

8 ounces semi-
  sweet chocolate
  chips (about
  1½ cups)

⅓ cup Guinness
  stout

Heat hot fudge sauce in a double-boiler until pourable. In a pot over very low heat, heat chocolate chips and Guinness together until chocolate has melted, then stir into hot fudge sauce. Mix well. Pour into a serving dish.

Refrigerate leftovers; reheat before serving.

Per ¼-cup serving:

271 calories

11g fat

36% calories from fat

6g saturated fat

1mg cholesterol

3g protein

40g carbohydrate

27g sugar

2.5g fiber

134mg sodium

46mg calcium

262mg potassium

TIRAMISU

AMICI'S > 210 North Kirkwood Road • Kirkwood • 314-821-2222 • amicisrestaurant.com

YIELD: 15 SERVINGS

38 ladyfingers, split (about 5 ounces; see note)

¾ cup Kahlua or Kamora coffee liqueur

¼ cup rum

13 egg yolks

1⅓ cups granulated sugar

1⅓ cups milk

2 pounds mascarpone or cream cheese, softened

3 cups heavy (whipping) cream

1 teaspoon vanilla

½ cup powdered sugar

1 pound chocolate, finely grated

1 to 2 tablespoons unsweetened cocoa powder

Line the bottom of a 9-by-13-by-2-inch baking pan with split ladyfingers; arrange remaining ladyfingers in a single layer on a shallow pan or tray. Stir together liqueur and rum; brush all of the ladyfingers with liqueur mixture. Continue brushing about every 10 minutes until all liquid is absorbed.

In a large, heavy saucepan, beat yolks lightly. Stir in granulated sugar and milk. Place over medium-high heat; cook until thickened, stirring constantly. Remove from heat and pour into a large bowl. Cover and refrigerate until cooled at least to room temperature, 1 to 2 hours. (For faster cooling, place the bowl in a larger bowl of ice and stir until cool.)

In the large bowl of an electric mixer, beat cheese at low speed until smooth; add cooled egg custard and beat until well mixed and completely smooth. Spread half of the custard mixture over ladyfingers in pan. Use a spatula or egg turner to lift second layer of soaked ladyfingers onto custard mixture, arranging to cover completely. Spoon on remaining custard mixture and smooth top. Refrigerate 15 minutes.

Whip cream with vanilla and powdered sugar until stiff. Spread over custard mixture; sprinkle with grated chocolate. Place cocoa powder in a fine strainer and dust generously over surface. Cover and refrigerate overnight.

Note: Use crispy Italian ladyfingers, called savoiardi. Do not use soft, cakelike ladyfingers.

Per serving:

852 calories
60g fat
63% calories from fat
34g saturated fat
347mg cholesterol
15g protein
56g carbohydrate
47g sugar
no fiber
135mg sodium
170mg calcium
149mg potassium

VERITAS BREAD PUDDING

VERITAS > 1722 Clarkson Road • Chesterfield • 636-530-9505 • veritasgateway.com

YIELD: 12 SERVINGS

16 to 20 small croissants

Butter, for greasing dish

1 cup sweetened dried cranberries, divided

½ cup chopped dried apricots, divided

9 eggs, lightly beaten

1½ cups whole milk

1½ cups heavy cream

¾ cup granulated sugar

1½ teaspoons ground cinnamon

1½ teaspoons freshly grated nutmeg

1 pinch salt

Tear croissants into pieces; you should have about 12 cups. Spread out on the counter to dry for 1 to 6 hours.

Preheat the oven to 350 degrees. Lightly butter a 9-by-13-inch glass baking dish; add croissant pieces to baking dish. Toss with about ¾ of the dried cranberries and apricots. Sprinkle remaining cranberries and apricots over croissant pieces. Ingredients should not be higher than rim of dish.

In a large bowl, blend together eggs, milk, cream, sugar, cinnamon, nutmeg and salt; pour over bread and fruit.

Use an egg turner to gently press bread into the egg/milk mixture, soaking the bread. (You should see wet bread, not bread floating.) Bake until golden brown on top and set in the center, about 1 hour. (A knife inserted in the center should come out clean.)

Variations:

• Use your choice of dried fruit.

• Use any variety of bread. Include the crust, which adds texture and color to the finished dish. (Try using cinnamon-raisin bread, pound cake or banana bread. No more than half should be whole-wheat bread, as it tends to make a heavy dessert.)

• During the winter holidays, use eggnog to replace some of the milk/cream mixture.

• For a lighter dessert, use skim milk and half-and-half instead of whole milk and cream.

• Top with ice cream and/or dessert sauces.

Per serving:

508 calories

28g fat

50% calories from fat

15g saturated fat

240mg cholesterol

11g protein

53g carbohydrate

30g sugar

3g fiber

497mg sodium

104mg calcium

252mg potassium

BREAD PUDDING

SQWIRES > 1415 South 18th Street • St. Louis • 314-865-3522 • sqwires.com

YIELD: 12 SERVINGS (SEE NOTE)

Butter, to grease pan

2 (1-pound) brioche loaves,
  cut into cubes

6 eggs

6 egg yolks

8 cups 40 percent "gourmet"
  whipping cream (see note)

3 cups granulated sugar

3 cups chopped fresh fruit
  (see note)

Preheat the oven to 300 degrees. Butter the bottom and sides of a 9-by-13-inch baking pan. Place bread cubes into the pan.

In a large bowl, mix together eggs, yolks, cream and sugar; stir until sugar is dissolved. Pour egg mixture over bread. Distribute fruit evenly over bread; let stand 10 minutes. Bake 20 minutes, then cover with foil and bake about 20 minutes more, just until liquid has set.

Let cool completely; cut into squares.

Notes: If desired, substitute ¼ to ½ cup liqueur for an equal amount of cream.

Use your choice of fresh fruit or fruit frozen without sugar. If desired, add a handful of nuts that complement the fruit, such as blueberries and almonds, peaches and hazelnuts or cherries and walnuts. This recipe may be halved and baked in a 7-by-10-inch pan.

Per serving (made with chopped peeled apples):

1,164 calories

80g fat

62% calories from fat

47g saturated fat

546mg cholesterol

16g protein

95g carbohydrate

58g sugar

1.5g fiber

393mg sodium

155mg calcium

189mg potassium

COCONUT CREAM DREAM CAKE

THE BLUE OWL RESTAURANT AND BAKERY > Second and Mill streets • Kimmswick • 636-464-3128 • theblueowl.com

YIELD: 1 (3-LAYER) CAKE, 12 SERVINGS

1½ (18.5-ounce) yellow "butter-recipe" cake mixes (1 mix plus 1⅞ cups)

½ cup (1 stick) butter, melted

1½ cups water

5 eggs

1 tablespoon vanilla

3 cups sour cream

1½ cups granulated sugar

4½ cups sweetened flaked coconut (about 18 ounces)

Preheat oven to 350 degrees. Grease and flour three 9-inch round cake pans.

Combine cake mix, melted butter, water, eggs and vanilla in the large bowl of an electric mixer. Beat until well blended (batter will be thick). Divide among prepared pans. (You will have about 3 cups of batter in each pan.) Bake according to directions on cake box, just until layers test done with a wooden pick. Let cool on wire racks.

If layers have developed rounded tops while baking, slice the crowns off two of the layers to make them more level. Trim the top layer or leave it rounded.

If any liquid is visible on sour cream, pour it off and discard. Combine sour cream, sugar and coconut in a large bowl; stir until sugar has dissolved.

Place one cake layer on a cake plate. Spread about one-fifth of the coconut cream evenly over the layer. Repeat with the second and third layers. Coat sides with remaining coconut cream. Store in refrigerator.

Per serving:

709 calories

33g fat

42% calories from fat

21g saturated fat

130mg cholesterol

8g protein

95g carbohydrate

65g sugar

3g fiber

580mg sodium

179mg calcium

200mg potassium

CHOCOLATE GOOEY BUTTER CAKE

McCORMICK AND SCHMICK'S > 17 West County Center • Des Peres • 314-835-1300 • mccormickandschmicks.com

YIELD: 12 LARGE SERVINGS

1 (18-ounce) devil's food
   cake mix

3 eggs, divided

1 cup (2 sticks) butter,
   melted, divided

1 pound powdered sugar
   (about 3¾ cups)

8 ounces cream cheese,
   softened

½ cup plus 2 tablespoons
   unsweetened cocoa
   powder, divided

1½ teaspoons vanilla

Preheat oven to 350 degrees (see note). Lightly grease a 9-by-13-inch metal pan.

To make the base, beat together cake mix, 1 egg and ½ cup melted butter just until combined. Press into prepared pan, pressing dough about ½ inch up the sides.

Set aside 2 tablespoons powdered sugar to use in the garnish. To make the filling, beat cream cheese with ½ cup cocoa powder, the remaining powdered sugar and vanilla in a large bowl. One at a time, beat in the remaining 2 eggs, then beat in remaining ½ cup melted butter. Beat until smooth, scraping down the sides of the bowl as necessary.

Spread the filling over the base. Bake just until set, about 25 minutes. Let cool completely.

Before serving, combine the remaining 2 tablespoons powdered sugar and cocoa powder. Spoon into a sieve; dust over the cake.

Note: Be sure that your oven is not more than 350 degrees. Use an oven thermometer if necessary. Cake is best served at room temperature. If you cut the cake into rounds, as in the photo, use leftover scraps in a sundae or trifle.

Per serving:

573 calories

29g fat

46% calories from fat

16g saturated fat

140mg cholesterol

7g protein

71g carbohydrate

54g sugar

2g fiber

440mg sodium

67mg calcium

160mg potassium

PEACH CAKES

ATLAS RESTAURANT > 5513 Pershing Avenue • St. Louis • 314-367-6800 • atlasrestaurantstl.com

YIELD: 8 SERVINGS

2 tablespoons butter, plus more to prepare ramekins

3 large peaches, peeled and cut into chunks (about 3½ cups)

1¼ cups granulated sugar, divided

¼ teaspoon lemon juice

1 cup all-purpose flour

½ teaspoon kosher salt

2 teaspoons baking powder

1 cup milk

Powdered sugar, for optional garnish

Preheat oven to 350 degrees. Butter eight 6-ounce ramekins; arrange on a heavy baking pan.

Combine peaches with ¼ cup sugar and lemon juice; set aside. Melt 2 tablespoons butter; set aside.

In a medium bowl, stir together remaining 1 cup sugar, flour, salt and baking powder. Combine milk and melted butter. While stirring, pour milk mixture into dry ingredients; stir until lumps disappear. Using a slotted spoon, add peaches to batter, discarding any liquid left in the bowl.

Ladle into prepared ramekins. Bake until golden brown on top, about 35 minutes. Let cool slightly, then unmold from ramekins. If desired, dust with powdered sugar before serving.

Per serving:

256 calories

4g fat

14% calories from fat

2.5g saturated fat

11mg cholesterol

3g protein

52g carbohydrate

39g sugar

1.5g fiber

255mg sodium

110mg calcium

204mg potassium

CARROT CAKE

FALCON DINER > Ameristar Casino • 1260 South Main Street • St. Charles • 636-940-4955 • ameristar.com

YIELD: 12 SERVINGS

For cake:

Vegetable shortening, to prepare pans

1½ cups all-purpose flour, plus more to prepare pans

1 cup granulated sugar

1 cup packed brown sugar

5 eggs

1½ cups vegetable oil

1 tablespoon baking soda

1 tablespoon plus 1 teaspoon baking powder

½ teaspoon salt

1 teaspoon ground cinnamon

9 ounces carrots, finely shredded (about 2½ cups)

1¼ cups chopped walnuts

For frosting and garnish:

3 (8-ounce) packages cream cheese, softened

½ cup (1 stick) butter, softened

3 cups powdered sugar

1 cup coconut, lightly toasted and cooled

To prepare cake: Coat three 8-inch-diameter cake pans (see note) with shortening; dust with flour and set aside. Preheat oven to 300 degrees.

In the large bowl of an electric mixer, combine granulated sugar, brown sugar, eggs and oil; beat 2 minutes at medium speed. Add 1½ cups flour, baking soda, baking powder, salt and cinnamon; beat 2 minutes, scraping bowl as needed. Add carrots and walnuts; beat 2 minutes.

Divide batter evenly among prepared pans. Bake about 40 minutes, until a wooden pick inserted near the center comes out clean. Let cakes cool 15 minutes, then turn out onto wire racks to cool completely.

To frost and garnish cake: Beat cream cheese, butter and powdered sugar together until smooth. Fill and frost cake. Coat sides of cake with toasted coconut, pressing firmly into frosting. Chill until serving time.

Note: The Falcon Diner's version of this dessert is a five-layer extravaganza garnished with frosting "carrots." This recipe makes enough batter for three 8-inch layers or two layers plus 12 cupcakes; bake cupcakes 30 to 35 minutes.

Per serving:

995 calories

67.5g fat

61% calories from fat

25g saturated fat

171mg cholesterol

11g protein

86g carbohydrate

69g sugar

2.5g fiber

817mg sodium

190mg calcium

333mg potassium

187

BAKED APPLE CUSTARD PIE

SHANGRI-LA DINER > 2201 Cherokee Street • St. Louis • 314-772-8308 • theshangriladiner.com

YIELD: 7 SERVINGS

For crust:

1¼ cups all-purpose flour

1 cup whole-wheat flour

6 tablespoons granulated sugar

1 teaspoon salt

1 cup (2 sticks) unsalted cold butter, cut into chunks

6 to 10 tablespoons apple cider

For filling:

⅓ cup granulated sugar

1 egg, lightly beaten

⅔ cup sour cream

2 teaspoons vanilla

3 tablespoons all-purpose flour

5 medium tart apples, unpeeled, cored and thinly sliced

For topping:

3 tablespoons brown sugar

3 tablespoons granulated sugar

1 teaspoon ground cinnamon

¾ cup chopped walnuts

To prepare crust: Sift together flours, sugar and salt. With a pastry blender or two table knives, cut in butter until mixture resembles rolled oats. Sprinkle with 6 tablespoons cider; mix until dough forms a ball, adding up 4 tablespoons more cider if necessary.

Cut off a third of the dough, cover and refrigerate. Roll out the remainder for a bottom crust; line a deep-dish glass pie plate, crimp the edges and set aside. Preheat the oven to 350 degrees.

To prepare filling: In a large bowl, stir together sugar, egg, sour cream, vanilla and flour. When well blended, add apples; toss to coat. Pour mixture into crust.

To prepare topping: In another bowl, blend together sugars, cinnamon and walnuts; sprinkle evenly over the filling.

Pinch off marble-size pieces of the reserved dough; arrange evenly on top of pie. Bake for 55 to 65 minutes, covering top with foil if necessary to prevent excess browning. Pie is done when juices are bubbly and apples are tender. Serve warm or cool.

Per serving:

722 calories

40g fat

50% calories from fat

20g saturated fat

109mg cholesterol

9g protein

81.5g carbohydrate

44g sugar

6g fiber

369mg sodium

75mg calcium

332mg potassium

CARROT COBBLER

FRAZER'S RESTAURANT & LOUNGE > 1811 Pestalozzi Street • St. Louis • 314-773-8646 • frazergoodeats.com

YIELD: 12 SERVINGS

For cobbler:

3 cups shredded carrots

3 cups granulated sugar, divided

2½ cups cake flour

2 tablespoons baking powder

2 teaspoons ground cinnamon

½ teaspoon ground ginger

1¾ cups milk

½ teaspoon vanilla

¼ cup pecans

¼ cup golden raisins

½ cup (1 stick) margarine or butter, melted

For vanilla cream sauce:

4 cups heavy cream, divided

2 tablespoons cornstarch

¼ cup granulated sugar

2 tablespoons vanilla

For caramel sauce:

1 cup granulated sugar

2 tablespoons light corn syrup

2 cups heavy cream

To prepare cobbler: Preheat the oven to 350 degrees.

In a large bowl, toss carrots with 1 cup sugar. Set aside. (Carrots will start to release their liquid.)

Stir together remaining 2 cups sugar, flour, baking powder, cinnamon and ginger; whisk in milk. Stir in vanilla, pecans and raisins.

Pour melted margarine into a 9-by-13-inch baking dish; add batter. Evenly top with the carrot mixture, pouring all the carrot's liquid over the batter. Bake about 45 minutes or until set in the center. (The carrots will sink to the bottom, and the batter will form a chewy cake-like crust.)

To prepare vanilla cream sauce: In a small bowl, stir together ¼ cup cream with cornstarch. Pour remaining 3¾ cups cream into a saucepan; add cornstarch mixture. Stir in sugar until dissolved. Cook over medium heat, stirring constantly, until sauce thickens slightly. Stir in vanilla.

To prepare caramel sauce: Combine sugar and corn syrup in a small saucepan. Cook over medium heat until mixture starts to turn golden brown; carefully add cream. Cook until blended and thickened.

Serve warm cobbler with vanilla cream sauce and a drizzle of caramel sauce.

Per serving:

959 calories

55g fat

52% calories from fat

30g saturated fat

167mg cholesterol

7g protein

109g carbohydrate

77g sugar

2g fiber

414mg sodium

278mg calcium

306mg potassium

CRÈME BRULÉE

LORUSSO'S CUCINA > 3121 Watson Road • St. Louis • 314-647-6222 • lorussos.com

YIELD: 6 SERVINGS

3 cups heavy (40 percent "gourmet") whipping cream

9 egg yolks, at room temperature

About ¾ cup granulated sugar, divided (see note)

1 teaspoon vanilla

1 pinch kosher salt

Fresh berries, for garnish

Powdered sugar, for garnish

Preheat oven to 275 degrees.

Place cream in a heavy stainless-steel or enamel pot. Place over medium heat.

Meanwhile, in a medium bowl, combine yolks, ½ cup sugar, vanilla and salt; whisk until thoroughly combined. When cream is very hot, stir about one-fourth of the cream into the egg mixture; mix well with a spatula. When the egg mixture is tempered (warmed), add it to the hot cream in the pot; remove from heat. Mix until well incorporated. (The custard should lightly coat the back of a spoon; if not, return to the stove and cook 4 or 5 minutes, stirring constantly.)

Divide mixture among six 8-ounce ovenproof ramekins or custard cups. Place ramekins in a 9-by-13-inch pan. Pour hot water into the pan until it reaches halfway up the ramekins.

Bake on the center oven rack for 45 to 50 minutes, until custard is set. Remove from oven, but leave ramekins in the water bath until cooled, about 30 minutes.

Remove ramekins from water bath. Refrigerate until cold, at least 2 hours, or up to 2 days.

Sprinkle about 2 teaspoons sugar over each custard. For best results, use a small, hand-held propane torch to caramelize the sugar, heating it just until it melts and browns. (A butane torch will work to caramelize the sugar, but propane is a cleaner gas. If you don't have a torch, you can place the ramekins under a hot broiler until the sugar melts and browns. This method warms the custard; chill until cold, then serve.)

Top each with fresh berries, dust with powdered sugar and serve immediately.

Note: You can substitute Splenda for the sugar in the custard, but you must use granulated sugar for the caramelized tops.

Per serving:

622 calories

50.5g fat

73% calories from fat

30g saturated fat

470g cholesterol

6g protein

36g carbohydrate

32g sugar

no fiber

77mg sodium

110mg calcium

118mg potassium

MOCHA MUFFINS

KALDI'S COFFEEHOUSE > multiple locations • kaldiscoffee.com

YIELD: 12 LARGE OR 20 REGULAR MUFFINS

¼ cup (2 shots) freshly extracted espresso (see note)

¾ cup plus 1½ teaspoons granulated sugar, divided

2 cups plus 2 tablespoons all-purpose flour

½ cup packed brown sugar

½ teaspoon ground cinnamon

1 teaspoon very finely ground coffee (espresso grind; should be powdery, not sandy)

1 teaspoon baking powder

1 teaspoon baking soda

1 teaspoon salt

½ cup sour cream

¼ cup milk

½ cup canola or vegetable oil

2 eggs, at room temperature, slightly beaten

1 tablespoon vanilla

12 ounces semi-sweet chocolate chips

Powdered sugar

Immediately after preparing espresso, stir in 1½ teaspoons granulated sugar. Let cool to room temperature. (The sugar will help keep the espresso from becoming bitter while cooling.)

For large muffins, preheat oven to 365 degrees. Line 12 Texas-size muffin cups with paper liners. For regular muffins, preheat oven to 375 degrees and line 20 standard (2¾-inch) muffin cups with paper liners.

In a large bowl, mix together flour, remaining ¾ cup granulated sugar, brown sugar, cinnamon, ground coffee, baking powder, baking soda and salt.

In another bowl, whisk together sour cream and milk. Add cooled espresso, oil, eggs and vanilla; whisk until well blended. Stir into flour mixture just until dry ingredients are incorporated. Do not overmix. Fold in chocolate chips.

Divide batter equally among prepared muffin cups. Bake Texas-size muffins 20 to 25 minutes, standard-size muffins 16 to 18 minutes or until tops spring back when touched gently. Immediately after baking, remove muffins from pan and place on rack to cool. Before serving, sprinkle with powdered sugar.

Note: If you don't have an espresso machine at home, you can buy espresso at a coffeehouse. Order a double espresso to go and stir a packet of sugar into it right away. You can substitute ¼ cup very strong coffee, but that will give the muffins a much milder coffee flavor.

Variation: For Dark-Chocolate Mocha Muffins, use dark brown sugar and add ¼ cup cocoa powder to the dry ingredients, stirring well to remove lumps. Decrease flour by 2 tablespoons.

Per regular muffin:

265 calories

12.5g fat

42% calories from fat

4.5g saturated fat

24mg cholesterol

3g protein

35g carbohydrate

23g sugar

1.5g fiber

222mg sodium

30mg calcium

108mg potassium

Per large muffin:

436 calories

20.5g fat

42% calories from fat

7g saturated fat

39mg cholesterol

5g protein

58g carbohydrate

38g sugar

2.5g fiber

369mg sodium

49mg calcium

180mg potassium

PUMPKIN BREAD

THE DAILY BREAD BAKERY AND CAFÉ > 11719 Manchester Road • Des Peres • 314-909-0010 • thedbcafe.com

YIELD: 2 LOAVES; ABOUT 20 SLICES

²/₃ cup canola oil

2²/₃ cups granulated sugar

4 large eggs

1 (15-ounce) can pumpkin

²/₃ cup water

3¹/₃ cups unbleached all-purpose flour

½ teaspoon baking powder

2 teaspoons baking soda

1½ teaspoons salt

1 teaspoon ground nutmeg

½ teaspoon ground cinnamon

1 teaspoon vanilla

Preheat the oven to 350 degrees. Lightly grease and flour two 9-by-5-inch loaf pans.

In the large bowl of an electric mixer, beat together oil and sugar. Beat in eggs, pumpkin and water. Add flour, baking powder, baking soda, salt, nutmeg, cinnamon and vanilla; mix well.

Spoon half the batter into each pan. Bake 1 hour or until a knife inserted near the center comes out clean. Let cool before removing from pans. If serving the next day, wrap in plastic.

Variation: For Pumpkin Praline Bread, stir together 1 cup chopped pecans, ½ cup packed brown sugar and 4 teaspoons melted butter; sprinkle over loaves before baking.

Per slice:

277 calories

9g fat

29% calories from fat

1g saturated fat

42mg cholesterol

4g protein

45g carbohydrate

28g sugar

1g fiber

328mg sodium

22mg calcium

81mg potassium

STRAWBERRY-APPLESAUCE BREAD

ALLAGHER'S > 114 West Mill Street • Waterloo • 618-939-9933 • gallagherswaterloo.com

YIELD: 2 LOAVES; 16 SLICES

2/3 cups cake flour, plus more to prepare pan

1/2 cups unsweetened or sweetened applesauce

cup strawberry preserves

eggs

cups granulated sugar

cup raisins

tablespoons butter, melted

1/4 teaspoons baking powder

1/4 teaspoons baking soda

1/4 teaspoons salt

1/2 teaspoons ground cinnamon

teaspoon ground cloves

cup chopped pecans

Preheat the oven to 350 degrees. Coat two 4-by-8-inch loaf pans (see tester's note) with cooking spray; line with parchment paper and spray again. Dust inside of pans with flour; set aside.

Combine 2⅔ cups flour, applesauce, preserves, eggs, sugar, raisins, melted butter, baking powder, baking soda, salt, cinnamon, cloves and pecans in mixer bowl; beat just until thoroughly blended. Do not overmix. Divide batter evenly between prepared pans.

Bake about 20 minutes. Carefully and slowly rotate pans in the oven to ensure even baking. (Do not jostle the bread, or it could fall.)

Bake about 25 minutes more or until the center is just set and a wooden pick inserted near the center comes out clean. This batter has a high proportion of sugar; watch closely so that bread does not burn.

Let breads cool in pans about 15 minutes. Lift parchment from pans; carefully peel paper from loaves. Let cool completely on racks.

Tester's note: Loaf pans vary slightly in size; if using a larger pan, reduce oven temperature to 325 degrees and bake until bread tests done as indicated.

Per slice:

268 calories

4g fat

13% calories from fat

1g saturated fat

43mg cholesterol

3g protein

55g carbohydrate

38g sugar

1g fiber

593mg sodium

56mg calcium

120mg potassium